Praise for Tr̶u̶ ... Old Sag Harbor

These columns are an enjoyable way to learn more about Sag Harbor's interesting history. It's always a delight to see Jim Marquardt's "Looking Back" essays in the *Express*.

> — Greg Ferraris, principal of GNFerraris LLC,
> former mayor of Sag Harbor

You are always in for a treat when the *Express* publishes one of Jim Marquardt's columns on the history of our Village. With his exceptional background and knowledge he provides the reader with an in-depth view of our rich history as he creates a vivid picture of what Sag Harbor was like during its early days.

Whether the topic is how the colonists affected the native Americans, adventures and stories of our whaling days, or stories of our local men and women who served in wars to protect our freedom, Jim presents the topic in a well researched manner that is both informative and entertaining. You might even read about one of your ancestors as I did when he wrote the column on David Frothingham, who published the first newspaper on Long Island, right here in Sag Harbor. It doesn't matter how many generations you've been here, it's always good reading when Jim dips his pen in the ink.

> — Jack Youngs, President, Sag Harbor Historical Society

The residents of Sag Harbor have a great appetite for history, and lord knows the village has witnessed plenty of historic moments, from the advent of whaling and the Battle of Sagg Harbor to the succession of factories that defined the village's economy through the 19th and 20th centuries. Over those few hundred years there have been dozens — hundreds — of stories worth telling and retelling, heroic and eccentric personalities to explore, tales of war and peace.

For the past ten years, Jim Marquardt has shared many of these stories with readers of *The Sag Harbor Express*. With this volume many more will enjoy his colorful retelling of the history of one of America's oldest villages, offering a window which looks back on a community that suffered and enjoyed the growing pains and unbridled hope of an evolving nation.

— Bryan Boyhan, former longtime editor and publisher of
The Sag Harbor Express. "

Far beyond being simply a compilation of well written essays, Jim's timely contribution lays out a history showing the authentic character of Sag Harbor. Congratulations.

— Ted Conklin, the American Hotel

True Stories of
Old Sag Harbor

Whaling Adventures, Indians and Colonists, Wars,
Shipwrecks, Writers and Artists

True Stories of Old Sag Harbor

Whaling Adventures, Indians and Colonists,
Wars, Shipwrecks, Writers and Artists

Enjoy!

Jim Marquardt

Columnist for the *Sag Harbor Express*

Harbor Electronic Publishing

New York | Sag Harbor

HEPDigital.com

2019

Jim Marquardt

ISBN (paper): 978-1-932916-27-0

ISBN (eBook): 978-0-9740201-9-8

Library of Congress Control Number: 2018964864

Printed in the United States of America.

A Note on the Type

This book is set in Minion Pro, an Adobe Originals typeface designed by Robert Slimbach. It was inspired by classical, old-style typefaces of the late Renaissance, a period of elegant, beautiful, and highly readable type designs. The display and caption font is Gill Sans. Designed by Eric Gill, it is the Helvetica of England: ubiquitous and utilitarian.

For my wife Ann

who makes everything better

Contents

Native Americans and Colonial Life 59

Sag Harbor in War 93

Living With the Sea   125

Business Enterprise   157

Introduction

Though a relatively small town, Sag Harbor on the East End of Long Island, New York, has a fascinating history. Members of the Algonquin Indian tribe lived and summered here thousands of years ago. English colonists arrived nearby in 1645, found the soil ideal for farming and established some of the earliest settlements in the New World.

At one time, Sag Harbor commerce was busier than New York City's and led to establishment of the first Custom House on Long Island. Sag Harbor may be best known as one of the leading whaling harbors on the East Coast. At the industry's height in the 1840s, it was home port for some 60 whaling ships that roamed the world's oceans, supported by the village's rope works, coopers, blacksmiths, sailmakers, and shipbuilders. Revenue from the industry built distinctive homes that still line Main Street. The first Long Island newspaper was published here in 1791.

The Revolutionary War and Civil War affected Sag Harbor and its people like hundreds of other small towns in young America. The end of whaling in the latter half of the 1800s brought a period of decline, other businesses unable to keep up with modern advancements. In later years, writers and artists began coming here for respite from the City, and a freer, less expensive lifestyle. Now, close to, but still separate in spirit from the fabled Hamptons, Sag Harbor attracts visitors from all over the world.

These stories which originally appeared in the *Sag Harbor Express* over the last ten years create an intimate picture of some of the events and people that created the unique personality of an "American Beauty."

The author thanks *Sag Harbor Express* Publisher Emeritus Bryan Boyhan for his guidance and encouragement. Bryan approached me some ten years ago on Main Street as he made his rounds to check on the state of the village. He saw something I wrote and suggested that maybe I should try a regular column for the *Express*.

He further suggested that I should concentrate on the history of the old whaling village. Having been thoroughly bored by history while in high school, I wasn't sure I wanted to sign up for the job. But once I got into it and realized the wealth of fascinating information about Sag Harbor, I became thoroughly engrossed and felt lucky to get the assignment.

We decided to title the columns "Looking Back" which gave me lots of leeway, I could write about something that happened a year ago, or centuries in the past. Since I'd only moved to the Harbor 15 years before, I knew I was still considered a newcomer. Researching the Sag Harbor of yesteryear gave me new appreciation for the village that Dorothy Zaykowski called "An American Beauty."

Now while walking on Main Street and seeing a few tourists standing on a corner (they're easy to spot), I often stop to talk and to launch into a description of the many wonderful features of the village. Maybe I'm kidding myself but they always seem to appreciate the information.

Jim Marquardt

Sag Harbor

December 2018

1

Sag Whalers Sailed the World

"Entombed in the Ocean"

An imposing, white marble shaft representing the broken mast of a ship stands tall in Sag Harbor's Oakland Cemetery off Jermain Avenue. The inscription on the base says simply "Entombed in the ocean, they live in our memory." The names of six Sag Harbor whaleship captains who lost their lives hunting the huge quarry in the far reaches of the oceans are engraved into the sides of the base:

> John E. Howell, master of the *France*, killed July 1840 "In an encounter with a sperm whale in the 28th year of his age." Captain William H. Pierson of the *American*, age 30, killed in the Pacific, June 1846. Captain Richard S. Topping of the *Thorn*, age 29, killed in the Atlantic, February 1838. Captain Alfred C. Glover, 29, of the *Acosta*, killed in the South Atlantic, January 1836. Captain Stratton H. Harlow, 27, of the *Daniel Webster*, killed in the Pacific, October 1938. Captain Charles W. Payne, 30, of the *Fanny*, killed in the South Atlantic, January 1838.

Sadly, the monument is missing the names of other captains in those years who never returned — a typhoon in the Pacific swept overboard Captain Ludlow of the *Governor Clinton*. Captain Howett of the *Telegraph* was lost near the Marquesas Islands. Captain Brown of the *Ontario* was killed during "cutting in," perhaps struck by one of the sharp, iron spades used in stripping blubber from a dead whale. (You can see these heavy tools in the Sag Harbor Whaling Museum.)

Some whales fought for their lives against their aggressors and actually attacked the whaleship and its boats. Alexander Starbuck writes in his *History of the American Whale Fishery* that the chief weapon of the right whale was its powerful tail which could smash and sink boats. The sperm whale used its toothed jaw or simply its great bulk. On a number of occasions a Sperm whale deliberately charged into a whaleship, most famously in the woeful tale of the *Essex* out of

Nantucket. An 85-foot whale twice attacked the 240-ton ship and sank her, forcing the crew into small boats. Adrift for months, the last survivors sustained themselves on the bodies of their dead shipmates. Herman Melville used the *Essex* as a source for his classic novel *Moby Dick*.

Male sperm whales normally grow over 60 feet long and weigh up to fifty tons. According to Eric Jay Dolin's book *Leviathan* they have the largest skull of any whale, the largest head of any animal, and the largest brain of any species. They can dive thousands of feet and stay underwater for an hour.

The Broken Mast monument in Oakland cemetery commemorates whaleship captains lost at sea.

When there weren't deaths, there were dozens of serious injuries. Captain Jacob Havens, born on Shelter Island, commander of the brig *America* and later the *Myra*, barely escaped the jaws of a sperm whale that crushed his whaleboat off the coast of Brazil. A glancing blow from the whale's teeth fractured his skull but he recovered with the help of a trephining operation at a Rio de Janeiro hospital, a risky procedure in the early days of surgery, over 150 years ago.

George Page made three voyages with Captain Havens on the *Myra*, had several battles with whales, and always managed to survive.

Once after a right whale broke his leg with a whip of its tail, he and the boat's crew tossed for hours in icy cold waves, clinging to their overturned whaleboat. Years later off the West African coast a big cow whale towed Page's whaleboat far out to sea until the exhausted beast finally succumbed. He and his boat crew lived on whale meat for four days, declaring it "nourishing if not exactly Delmonico fare." An English frigate picked up the lost sailors and returned them to the *Myra* off the mouth of the Congo River.

Before becoming a ship's master, James R. Huntting was a boat steerer. When a sperm whale smashed and capsized his boat, he came up under it, tangled in line. He succeeded in freeing himself and rose to the surface, but a loop of the line attached to the sounding whale caught his ankle and dragged him under. He thought his life was over but when the whale slackened its plunge, he was able to pull himself forward and with his sheath knife cut the line below his foot. Huntting popped above water, nearly drowned and with a broken ankle. Patched up crudely on the ship, he limped for the rest of his life.

One of the names on the Oakland Cemetery monument is Richard Topping, master of the *Thorn*. When a whale stove in his boat, he jumped into the mate's boat and continued the pursuit. Topping, the mate and five crewmen never returned, no one left alive to describe their final struggle.

Robert R. Newell in *The Grisly Side of Whaling* compiled a grim accounting of the hazards that killed sailors during the heydays of the whaling industry. Eleven crewmen fell to their deaths while working aloft in the tall rigging. Natives on remote tropical islands slew 66 officers and crew members. Thirty-six men died from scurvy and 75 from other ailments. Thirty-three captains — at least nine from Sag Harbor — were killed by whales along with 71 mates and 242 crewmen. Thirty-six were dragged under by fouled lines and four men were killed while cutting in. In all, 386 sailors died fighting whales and 602 lives were taken by drowning and accident.

Starbuck writes that between 1800 and 1876, 368 whaling vessels were lost, foundering in gales and hurricanes, wrecked on often uncharted shores, destroyed by fire or crushed by Arctic ice. In the 21st century there may be a temptation to look back on whaling as a picturesque, even glorious part of Sag Harbor history. But the deaths and maiming of countless sailors, and the heartbreak it brought to families waiting years for their return, proved whaling to be an arduous and dangerous business.

Captains Courageous

Visitors to Sag Harbor might think that the celebration of our whaling heritage is little more than a promotion to attract tourists. But what they and no doubt some of our own residents don't realize is that during the first half of the nineteenth century, whaling was one of the largest industries in the United States and our small village was an important part of it. Today we would be ashamed to kill these mighty creatures, but 200 years ago few people even thought of conservation.

In 1847, thirty-two Sag Harbor whaling ships brought back 4,000 barrels of sperm oil, 64,000 barrels of whale oil, and 600,000 pounds of baleen — providing raw materials for candles, soap, lubricants, paint, oil lamps, hoop skirts, corsets and brushes. (The latter three items used baleen, a tough, fibrous, web-like material in the mouth of the whale that enabled it to filter plankton and other minute edibles from the sea.) In pursuing the whales that supplied this abundance, Sag Harbor captains navigated their vessels thousands of miles into remote reaches of the Atlantic and Pacific Oceans, often on voyages that lasted three or four years.

Thomas Welcome Roys (or Royce), a thirty-two year old in command of the whaleship *Superior*, was the first captain to sail north from the Pacific through the Bering Strait into the Arctic Ocean where he found great pods of Bowhead whales. He hadn't divulged his daring plan to the ship owners and crew for fear of being stopped, but a few years before, while recuperating in Siberia from an altercation with a Right whale, he had learned from a Russian naval officer that whales were plentiful in that frigid region.

He made his decision to sail far north after hunting fruitlessly in the South Atlantic for nearly a year. Despite the Arctic's strong currents, fog and rough seas, *Superior* chased whales around the clock, the sun never setting in summer that far north. Captain Roys and his crew took eleven bowheads, rendered their blubber in try-pots aboard the ship and loaded 1600 barrels of oil into the hold.

Our Sag Harbor Whaling Museum displays much more about Roys amazing life, including a detailed account of his Bering Sea voyage. Sadly, Roy's wife Marie Salliord, tired of his long absences at sea, took their three children and ran away with a former shipmate.

Captain Mercator Cooper of the whaleship *Manhattan* out of Sag Harbor, voyaging in the Pacific in 1847, went ashore on a deserted island off the coast of Japan to catch turtles for the crew's food supply. He came across eleven frightened Japanese sailors who had been shipwrecked. Though Japan barred foreign vessels from entering its waters, he decided to bring the sailors to their country. When he dropped anchor in the Bay of Jeddo within a couple of miles of the Imperial City, hundreds of armed boats surrounded *Manhattan*. High ranking Japanese officers came aboard and demanded to know why Cooper had trespassed.

When they realized he was on a peaceful rescue mission, they rewarded him with new spars, water, rice and fresh vegetables. After a week the Japanese ordered him to leave and never to visit Japan again, under penalty of death. The *Manhattan* was the first foreign ship to enter safely into Japanese waters. Many years and many adventures later, Mercator Cooper died at Barranquilla, Columbia, on April, 1872.

Isaac Ludlow, born in Bridgehampton, went to sea at age fifteen and in the following thirty-five years made twenty voyages on whaling ships, eight of them as master. In 1835, he rescued over 100 passengers and crew from the British ship *Meridian* wrecked in the Indian Ocean. The British Admiralty thanked him with a gold medal.

His most challenging adventure occurred while he was captain of the Sag Harbor bark *Oscar*. He gave the crew shore liberty during August 1845 in the port of Ilha Grande in South America. They came back to the ship drunk and in a vengeful mood for grievances they claimed to suffer during the voyage south. A mutinous gang came aft and one Curtis, the leader, ascended the ladder to the poop deck hefting an axe in his hand. When he refused an order to halt, Captain Ludlow hurried to his cabin, grabbed a rifle and went back on deck where he shot and killed Curtis, ending the mutiny.

The American consul ordered the whaleship's return to Sag Harbor where Ludlow was taken to New York City for trial. He was acquitted of the charge of murder. Dorothy Zaykowski wrote a somewhat different account of the incident in her book *Sag Harbor: An American Beauty*. Captain Ludlow and his wife Phebe and their three children rest in Bridgehampton's Old Burial Ground.

Captain James Huntting stood six-feet six-inches, weighed 250 pounds and was described as having "almost colossal proportions." Once while he was riding in a carriage, the reins parted and the horse broke away. Huntting reportedly grabbed the rear wheels by the spokes and brought the carriage to a halt.

According to *Leviathan, The History of Whaling in America* by Eric Jay Dolin, a major challenge aboard any ship was massive injury to a crewman. While Huntting was in command of a Sag Harbor whaleship, one of his boatmen became tangled in a line and was violently pulled from a whaleboat, losing four fingers from one hand and a foot nearly severed at the ankle. While others in the crew turned away in horror, Huntting strapped the injured crewman to a plank, amputated the foot and dressed the mangled hand. The treatment stabilized the sailor long enough for the ship to reach Hawaii and a hospital. Huntting left the sea in 1869 and went into the mercantile business with Nathan Tiffany in Bridgehampton.

These were a few of the iron men who sailed in wooden ships out of Sag Harbor.

✳ ✸ ✳

Success and Tragedy of Sag Harbor's Most Famous Whaling Captain

Thomas Welcome Roys was Sag Harbor's, and arguably America's, most remarkable whaleship captain. He was the first to sail north through the Bering Strait into the Arctic Ocean. He conceived a rocket-powered harpoon to hunt the biggest prey. He developed land-based try-works in remote parts of the world that extracted more oil from whale carcasses. He wrote a book that studied 18 types of cetaceans. And he was one of the first to realize that over-fishing could endanger the whales' survival. Tragically, he died penniless in a tiny Mexican town, depending on the kindness of strangers for a decent burial.

According to Schmitt, De Jong, and Winter, co-authors of an eponymous book about Roys (sometimes spelled Royce), he was born on a farm in Pultneyville, NY in 1816. At age 17 he shipped out on the Sag Harbor whaler *Hudson* under Captain Henry Green. His first chase off the Cape Verde Islands fascinated him and he signed on for voyages on *Gem*, *Josephine*, *Superior* and *William F. Safford*. In 1841, now 25 years old, he became skipper of the Sag whaler *Crescent*. Captain

Green must have approved of him because in August 1843 Roys married the captain's daughter Ann Eliza.

While recovering from an altercation with a whale in the northern Pacific, he learned about Arctic Ocean whales from a Russian seaman. Later on a long voyage aboard the *Superior*, after failing to find whales in the southern Pacific Ocean, Roys headed north for the Bering Strait and the Arctic. Those seas were so unexplored and so daunting at the time that his first mate Jim Eldridge burst into tears when he learned of their destination.

Fortunately bowhead whales in the Arctic proved easy prey and *Superior* returned to Sag Harbor in May 1849, after 21 months at sea, loaded with oil and baleen worth $100,000. Even the British Lords of the Admiralty recognized his daring feat. Most crewmen considered Roys "stable, fair and just," yet he obviously ran a tight ship. In Valparaiso during another voyage, on Christmas Eve he hauled on deck the ring leader of six malcontents and ordered him flogged. In San Francisco he turned over the mutineers to a U.S. Navy ship.

Roys and several friends bought the Sag whaler *William F. Safford* and outfitted her with special harpoon guns he had designed. Untested and untried, one of the guns misfired during an exploratory voyage in 1856 and blew away Roys' left hand. A couple of months later, he was chasing whales again and borrowing money to work on endless improvements of his invention. Even after killing whales, another major problem was their tendency to sink, so Roys went about devising gear to raise sunken whales, though their huge weights proved too much for the mechanism.

Roys started chasing whales in the North Atlantic and while visiting Lorient, France, met and married Marie Salliord, Ann Eliza having died in childbirth. Years later, Marie reportedly ran off with one of Roys shipmates. After much trial and error, and borrowing from investors, Roys's rocket-propelled harpoon gun evolved into a seven-foot long, shoulder-fired weapon, something like a World War II bazooka. (The Sag Harbor Whaling Museum owns a model of the launcher, and holds many of his logs and papers.) He partnered with Gustavus Adolphus Lilliendahl, a pyrotechnic manufacturer, and their innovations were considered the link between old and new style whaling. A Norwegian, Sved Foyn, and O. C. Hammer, a Dane, won great success with their own cannon designs and Roys' new venture petered out. Making matters worse, with the discovery of petroleum, the whaling business was declining.

But Roys never gave up. The *Sag Harbor Corrector*, March 10, 1866, reported the success of his Sag ship *Reindeer* in catching giant blue whales. Roys and two of his brothers manufactured and tried to market their new equipment, despite what the *Corrector* called the "crochetical" attitude of old-time seamen.

Roys was unheard of for many years, then turned up in 1876 in San Diego, worn out by a lifetime of long voyages, financial reversals, and failure of his inventions. He joined a ship but had contracted yellow fever and was put ashore at Mazatlan, Mexico. He was found "in the street, sick, destitute and wandering in mind" by American doctor D. M. Brown who took him into his own home. Roys died of a stroke a week later, on January 29, 1877, leaving only a roll of papers in his pocket. American Consul E. G. Kelton collected $60 from friends to bury the indefatigable but unfortunate Thomas Welcome Roys.

King of the South Seas

When Sag Harbor men shipped out on a whaleship, they quickly found out it wasn't a luxury cruise. They slept on crude bunks in a jammed forecastle, the food was inedible, and a rough captain and mate could make their lives miserable. And then there was the chance of being bashed by the flip of a whale's tail. So when a ship called at one of the South Seas islands in the Pacific, it's not surprising that sailors gazed with wonder at the palm fringed beach, the scantily clad native girls waving on the shore, and fresh food you could pluck from a tree or out of the lagoon.

Harry B. Sleight's *The Whale Fishery on Long Island*, published in 1931, tells the stories of several Sag Harbor men who succumbed to the temptations of these exotic islands, deserted their ships and lived long lives among hospitable natives. We can assume they had few ties in Sag Harbor and perhaps remembered tough Northeast winters.

As late as 1890 a visitor to the Navigator Islands (now the Samoan Islands) found that "the chief of the island, father and grandfather of a stalwart race of halfbreeds," was none other than Tom Seaman of Sag Harbor. He had shipped out from New Bedford on the *Albatross* in the 1830s, and when the ship touched the Polynesian Islands, probably to acquire fresh food, he and a pal slipped over the side, swam ashore and were hidden by native women when ship officers came looking for them. His shipmate pined away and died, but Seaman settled in nicely and many years later, at age 75, was discovered living contentedly with his wives in a hut near the beach.

Charles Nordhoff, who later collaborated with James Norman Hall in writing *Mutiny on the Bounty*, shipped aboard a Sag Harbor whaler and wrote about it in his book *Whaling and Fishing*. Compare life in the "hut near the beach" to his description of work on a whaler.

> The flames, darting high above the try-works revealed the masts, rigging and decks, in an unearthly glare, among which the men jumping or sliding about decks on their various duties seemed like demons dancing about an incantation fire.... The smell of the burning cracklings is too horribly nauseous for description. It is as though all the ill odors in the world were gathered together and being shaken up. Walking upon deck has become an impossibility...the safest mode of locomotion is sliding from place to place, on the seat of your pantaloons.

Sam Brant of Sag Harbor deserted from a whaler at the Bay of Islands off the northern tip of New Zealand, married and lived ashore until a war broke out. He moved to Auckland, took another native wife and lived with Fijians until missionaries came. Apparently they disapproved of his lifestyle so he next jumped to the Sandwich Islands (now Hawaiian Islands), and in 1894 was living in Honolulu.

Perhaps the most successful of the former Sag Harbor whalemen was actually from Shelter Island. In January of 1877, the *San Francisco Chronicle* reported,

> The *Ada May*, on her up trip, touched at Quiro Island [now Swains Island], where the celebrated and venerable Eli Jennings, an American patriarch, is like Robinson Crusoe, master of all he surveys....[Quiro] is some 200 miles north-northeast of the Samoan group. It is owned entirely by the patriarch, who has been there over thirty years. Mr. Jennings is married to a Samoan woman, and has a large family. He is well-to-do and happy as a lord."

Entrepreneurs and American Overseas Expansion published in 1994 says Jennings deserted from a whaling voyage in the Pacific and claimed to have gained ownership of the atoll from a British captain, moving there with his wife Malia in 1856. One American said "the best of them (the beachcombers) have lost their grip on civilization." The men collected bêche-de-mer, a kind of sea cucumber sold to China, as well as pearls and pearl shells along the shore, a surprisingly prosperous business. Sleight wrote,

> The pearl shell trade has been and is most profitable, and as no plant is required, the beachcombers and natives...can always be sure of ready money without any outlay, for the food they use is found in abundance on the scene of their labor."

We don't know how many Sag Harbor men chose the South Seas over Long Island. We would guess not too many; it would have been a huge step in the life of a young sailor to leave his family and homeland, even with its miserable winters.

✳ ✳ ✳

Sail Into Tokyo Harbor

In 1825, the Japanese government reaffirmed its National Seclusion Policy originally enacted in 1639. Simply stated, "Don't dare come here." Except for the Dutch who enjoyed a commercial treaty with them, the Japanese warned away all ships from western nations, especially whalers who sailed too close to their shores. In *Moby Dick*, Ishmael commented, "If that double-bolted land…is ever to become hospitable, it is the whaleship alone to which the credit will be due…." Commodore Matthew Perry's entry to Japanese waters in 1853 with an American naval fleet earned him a place in history books. Yet eight years earlier, the Sag Harbor whaleship *Manhattan*, commanded by Captain Mercator Cooper, entered Jeddo (later Tokyo) Harbor and spent several days in sometimes friendly, sometimes threatening contact with the Japanese.

The incident is wonderfully detailed in an article by C. F. Winslow in *The Friend*, a newspaper published in Honolulu in February 1846. Dr. Winslow, a missionary, interviewed Captain Cooper when *Manhattan* stopped in Hawaii. In April 1845 *Manhattan* was sailing towards the whaling regions of the northern Pacific Ocean when it passed uninhabited St. Peter's Island southwest of Japan. Captain Cooper decided to go ashore to capture turtles to provide fresh meat for his crew. Walking inland, he discovered eleven shipwrecked Japanese fishermen and, seeing their bedraggled state, offered to take them back to their homeland. On the voyage there, Cooper came upon a sinking fishing junk and rescued eleven more seamen. Reaching the Japanese coast, he sent a couple of the castaways ashore to explain to the Emperor his peaceful intentions.

As he neared Jeddo Bay, he was met by a barge carrying an officer of "rank and consequence" who told him he had the Emperor's permission to enter the harbor. Intensely curious about the Americans, a number of Japanese of all ranks, including the Governor of Jeddo and officers of the Emperor "arrayed in golden and gorgeous tunics" came aboard. They were especially fascinated by the Black crewmen aboard *Manhattan*, including Pyrrhus Concer and Gad Williams. Using a little English and many gestures, an interpreter told Cooper that no one was allowed off the ship under pain of death, "drawing a naked sword across the throat." Guards were posted and the *Manhattan*'s weapons confiscated while in the harbor. "Nearly a thousand" boats armed with lances and "steel weapons" ringed the *Manhattan* as the rescued Japanese seamen bade a tearful farewell to their American saviors.

Later, intending to repair one of his whaleboats, Cooper started lowering it from davits into the water alongside the ship. Thinking the Americans were planning to go ashore, the Japanese guards immediately drew swords, their officer declaring they would be slain and his own head would be in danger. But once he understood Cooper's ordinary purpose, he ordered his men to help with the work. The Emperor sent the Sag Harbor captain "wood, water, rice, rye in the grain, vegetables…and some crockery of the lacquered ware of the country."

A 1912 edition of *Southampton Magazine* said the Japanese also sent aboard a quantity of giant radishes. Emissaries told Cooper that the Emperor thought well of his "heart" and wanted him treated kindly, but added he "must not come again." It was early spring and Cooper admired what he could see of the Japanese mainland, every acre highly cultivated, the steeper hills terraced, presenting the appearance of hanging gardens. Cooper described the people as "short, square-built

and solid…of a light, olive complexion…intelligent, polite and educated." Common citizens wore wide trousers and loose, blue cotton
shirts, while dignitaries "were clothed in rich silks, embroidered with
gold and silken threads of various colors." The Japanese were par-
ticularly curious about the woolen garments of the Americans and
requested small samples to take ashore.

The Governor of Jeddo and other officers asked about America and
Cooper described his country's honorable character and its interest
in trade. After four days, the Governor ordered hundreds of sculling
boats to tow the *Manhattan* out to sea where Cooper spread his sails
and continued the hunt for whales in the northern ocean.

Months later, homeward bound, *Manhattan* sold her cargo of oil
and whalebone in Amsterdam, Holland. The last entry in the ship's
log read, "Cruise 2 yrs, 11 mos, 5 days."

The Japanese sailors inadvertently left aboard the *Manhattan* a
detailed chart of Japan and a notebook depicting the Empire's her-
aldry. If discovered the mistake could have cost them their heads.
The indefatigable Mercator Cooper brought these priceless me-
mentos home and some years later his descendants donated them
to the New Bedford Whaling Museum in Massachusetts. Cooper's
Southampton residence still stands, serving now as an annex to the
Rogers Memorial Library.

Gold Fever Struck Harbor Whalers

When gold was discovered at Sutter's Mill near San Francisco in 1848, the mad dash of prospectors from across the country — and from Europe, Asia, Latin America, even the Sandwich Islands — brought huge business and cultural changes. From a small settlement of 200 people in 1846, San Francisco boomed with 90,000 arrivals in 1849. In 1852, 20,000 people came from China alone. By 1853, Levi Strauss was selling denim overalls to gold miners. Mark Twain and Bret Harte wrote about them, Puccini featured them in his opera *The Girl of the West*. New steamboat lines and railroads carried thousands afflicted with gold fever; easterners trekked cross-country or sailed five to eight months around Cape Horn. They raced ashore, vessels abandoned at the docks converted into warehouses, stores, taverns, hotels, and eventually landfill for the bulging city. Many were whaleships from Sag Harbor, their crews caught up in the frenzy.

According to James Truslow Adams, in his 1962 book *Memorials of Old Bridgehampton*, the bones of Sag Harbor ships *Sabina*, *Cadmus*, and *Niantic* lie under the city of San Francisco. The loss of experienced sailors brought Sag Harbor's whaling industry almost to a standstill. Over 250 whaler crewmen left from Southampton Town alone. A lucky few amassed small fortunes, but none realized the riches that had tempted them away. Only a few years earlier, in the heyday of whaling, 60 vessels called Sag Harbor their home port. By 1849 only two ships embarked in a hunt for whales.

A group of men from Sag Harbor and the Hamptons formed The Southampton and California Mining and Trading Company in January 1849. Of the 60 stockholders, 50 sailed to California on the *Sabina*. Among them were 19 whaling captains. The *Sag Harbor Corrector* on February 14, 1849 published a list of those aboard, names familiar to anyone who has delved into village history:

David Hand, Peter Howell, Edward W. Halsey, D. B. Glover, Jedediah Conklin, Albert Hildreth, Augustus Ludlow, Franklin C. Jessup, William L. Huntting, Job Hedges, Robert E. Gardner, Stephen B. French, Howell Corwith.

Pyrrhus Concer came too, the veteran Black crewman who, a few years earlier aboard Mercator Cooper's vessel, brought shipwrecked Japanese sailors into Tokyo Bay. Other famous whalemen who tried their luck in the gold fields of California included captains N. R. Dering, John and Eli Fordham, William Topping, Elihu Pierson, Albert Jagger, and the ill-fated Thomas Welcome Roys.

Letters from Jagger found in the attic of the family home many years later describe the life of the adventurers. After reaching San Francisco, he wrote "The harbour on account of the amount of shipping and hurry and bustle...resembled N.Y. on the Pacific.... The buildings are of the frailest and cheapest kind. A great many businesses operate under large tents.... We have got through stripping the ship pretty well and shall probably start as soon as Monday for the diggin's."

Later he wrote from Steep Canyon, Bear River:

> Here we are in...a kind of wilderness, hemmed in with mountains and forests that a short time ago were inhabited only by wild beasts and human beings scarcely less wild.... We have a tier of logs rolled up, enclosing a space about as large as a common-sized pig pen, one end of which answers (with a few large stones laid up against the logs) for a fireplace and the other to spread down quilts, blankets to sleep upon.... The roof is an old tent suspended over the ridge pole and nailed to the logs upon the side.... We sometimes have venison or beef.... In addition to this we have porridge occasionally and now and then we have boiled potatoes or dried apples stewed for sauce.

In January 1850, the gold rush was already abating and he wrote, "There is gold here plenty and no mistake, but where one makes a fortune at mining, nine others will fail at it…." On September 28, 1851, the end was near. "There is a tremendous rush for home this fall, almost as great as 1849 and '50 to get out here."

Once the "forty-niners" were back home, they tried to resume the whaling trade, but the discovery of petroleum, the dwindling stock of whales, and the arrival of electricity towards the end of the century made its demise inevitable. They struggled on for years, but the sailors who worked the ships, as well as the village's rope works, coopers, riggers, shipwrights, blacksmiths, warehouses, and other support businesses suffered the decline of whaling, and Sag Harbor's economy fell into a long slump.

Scrimshaw — American Folk Art

We imagine whaling crews constantly in action — chasing their huge prey, trimming sails, swabbing the decks, dancing the hornpipe. They did all that — well, maybe not the dancing. But those jobs took up only a fraction of their day. Like men at war, whaling mixed moments of excitement and fright with long stretches of boredom. One source claims that a whaling expedition of a couple of years' duration might average only one whale kill a month. Finding an engrossing pastime to occupy monotonous days at sea is how scrimshaw came to be. It is now highly valued, one of the few original American folk arts.

The ivory teeth of sperm whales were the most prized medium for scrimshaw and the one you probably know best. A sperm whale might have 50 cone-shaped teeth, from four to ten inches long. The captain or mate would parcel them out to crew members. Every sailor

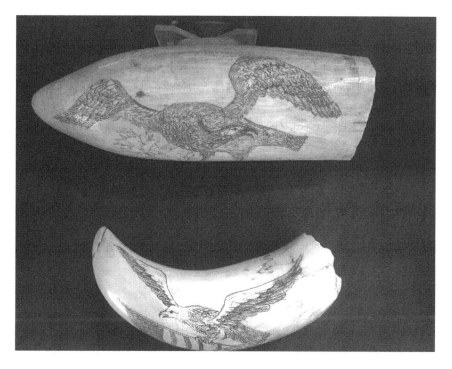

Etching scrimshaw scenes passed the time for sailors.

carried a jackknife and they used them to carve scenes onto the teeth. Heavy sailcloth needles scratched fine lines on the tooth for shading and dimension. Since the sailors were not trained artists, they would often place a picture from a magazine onto the tooth surface as a template, pierce a series of dots with the needle to outline the picture, then remove the template and connect the dots. India inks, lampblack or tobacco juice added color.

Scrimshaw usually wasn't made to sell, but was created for family members and sweethearts at home. Favorite etchings on sperm teeth were clipper ships under full sail and active scenes of furious whales and splintered boats. Women's figures symbolized "Liberty" and "America" in patriotic compositions. *Scrimshaw, Folk Art of the Whalers*, published by Walter Earle in 1957, shows a tooth etched with a drawing of the *Concordia*, a bark that sailed out of Sag Harbor. Underneath the etching was the name "Gorge (sic) Penney" who probably was the artist. The Sag Harbor Whaling Museum displays a collection of ivory scrimshaw, along with decorative and useful bone carvings made from the lower jawbone of sperm whales.

The next most popular medium were lower jawbones of the sperms which could be huge. (A jawbone frames the entrance to the Whaling Museum.) They were left on deck for a month or more to be cleaned and whitened by the weather. Jigsaws cut the jawbones into workable sizes depending on intended uses.

One popular item was a jagging wheel, a culinary tool up to ten inches long that was a pie-crimper and cookie edger. It had a long handle, a fluted wheel at one end and a fork on the other. Another feat of painstaking carving were swifts, collapsible latticework apparatus that women at home used to wind yarn for spinning and knitting. Sailors also carved skeletal bone into cribbage boards, chess pieces, canes, knife handles, and dozens of other implements.

We've all heard of "baleen" which sailors referred to as whale bone, but that's a misnomer. Unlike sperm whales, other species including blue, bowhead, minke, and humpback have no teeth. They feed by straining small fish and plankton from sea water through a series of baleen plates made of keratin, the same material in your hair and nails. Baleen plates hang from the upper jaws of these whales and become frayed into bristles that form a matted sieve. The material is light, strong, highly flexible, and easily cut into strips or molded into complex shapes. Common items made in plastic today — like pocket combs and brushes — were made of baleen in the early 19th century. Another commercial use was as stays in women's corsets which inspired a saucy sailor to write:

> In many a gale, has been the whale in which this bone did rest.
> His time is past, his bone at last must now support thy brest.

Generally the scrimshawed tooth or bone fell into several categories — ornamental, utilitarian, personal trinkets and play. Utilitarian was the largest purpose for bone, from working tools like belaying pins to all kinds of carpenter's tools and household items such as swifts, jagging wheels, knives and forks, rolling pins and boxes. Personal trinkets might be rings, bracelets and necklaces made from ivory and bone. Play items of bone included checker and cribbage boards, often inlayed, and children's toys.

Black Sailors Crewed the Whale Ships

On the wall of the Eastville Community Historical Society on Hampton Street is a modestly framed roster of "19th Century Eastville Whalers," the ships they sailed on, and their crew assignments. A little research revealed that the thirteen men listed were only a fraction of the thousands of African-Americans who manned ships that sailed from Sag Harbor, New Bedford, Nantucket and Greenport, pursuing their giant quarry throughout the Atlantic, Pacific, and Arctic Oceans. White and Black sailors joined rainbow crews of Shinnecock Indians, Pacific Islanders, Creoles, Peruvians, West Indians, Colombians, and a few Europeans. At sea, skin color was far less important than courage and skill, and the only measure of a shipmate was seamanship and success at catching whales. One Black seaman in those days said, "A colored man is looked upon as a man, and is promoted in rank according to ability to perform the same duties as the white man."

Sag Harbor whalers came upon great adventures. Pyrrus Concer, a steerman and harpooner was aboard the *Manhattan*, commanded by Mercator Cooper, when it rescued eleven shipwrecked fishermen near Japan in 1846. Captain Cooper decided to return the sailors to their homeland, though foreign vessels were forbidden to enter Japanese waters. Reaching port in the Bay of Jeddo, armed boats surrounded the *Manhattan* and Japanese officials demanded an explanation for the intrusion. The Japanese were intrigued with Concer, never having seen a Black man before. When they understood the Americans' peaceful purpose, the Japanese rewarded Cooper with spars, water, rice and fresh provisions, then ordered the *Manhattan* to leave and never to return. (A few years later, Concer joined the gold rush to California, but soon came back and in retirement sailed excursions around Lake Agawam in Southampton.)

In the golden age of whaling from 1800 to 1860, according to *Black Hands, White Sails* by Pat McKissack, African-Americans made up at least 25 percent of whaleship crews, and after the Civil War, as white sailors found jobs ashore, the numbers grew to 50 percent. Work on a whaleship was tough, smelly and dangerous, and voyages to the far reaches of the oceans might go on for two or three years. McKissack says whaling's death rate was second only to mining.

A young sailor wrote, "There is no class of men in the world who are so unfairly dealt with, so oppressed, so degraded, as the seamen who man the vessels engaged in the American whale fishery." We'd like to think ships out of Sag Harbor took a more enlightened approach to their crews, but that's probably unrealistic. The heydays of whaling coincided with the years of slavery in the United States and many Black crewmen were escaped slaves who took any job under any conditions. On a whaleship they were safe from slave hunters.

According to the *Long Island Historical Journal*, when *Fair Helen* departed Sag Harbor in 1817, her crew included Black sailors Cato Rogers and Nananias Cuffee. The *Abigail* shipped out a year later with six Black whalers, and in 1819 there were seven African-Americans in a crew of fifteen. They served as steermen-harpooners, stewards, cooks, seamen and greenhands. A few became mates and masters.

In 2000, the Sag Harbor Whaling Museum and Eastville Community Historical Society mounted a celebration of Black whalers. One of the exhibits was a heavy canvas "ditty bag" that belonged to Black boat-steerer Clayton King who shipped out from Sag Harbor in 1865 on the *Odd Fellow*, and in 1868 on the *Myra*. The ditty bag held a marlinspike and fid for splicing rope, a jackknife, a ball of beeswax to coat needles, and a "palm" of leather fitted with a metal socket and thumb hole for mending sails.

Isaiah Peake was a cook aboard the Sag Harbor bark *Oscar* under the command of Isaac Ludlow of Bridgehampton. While the ship was anchored off Rio de Janeiro, a drunken crewman named Curtis instigated a mutiny. When Curtis came at Ludlow with an axe, the captain shot him, ending the mutiny. A New York court tried the mutineers and sentenced Peake to only eight months in prison, probably realizing he was more a bystander than a mutineer.

Whaling was a major U.S. industry in the first half of the 19th century, producing basic ingredients for oil lamps, soap, smokeless candles, machine lubricants, bristles for brushes and brooms, bones for hoop skirts, corsets, and umbrella frames. Crew compensation was calculated in the form of "lays," a percentage share of the returning whaleship's valuable cargo. Owners took 50 percent, captains 12 percent. A green hand might get less than a half-percent before "expenses" were deducted to cover cash advances, clothing from the ship's slop chest, tobacco, and equipment. After months and years at sea some sailors owed money to the ship owners.

When the whaling industry began to decline, many ships sailed for the California coast where gold was discovered. One of them, the *Sabina*, with Black seaman John Crook aboard, took six months to reach the West Coast. In those times, square-rigged ships had to sail thousands of miles south along two continents, west around turbulent Cape Horn, and thousands of miles north to California. Like many others, *Sabina*'s crew deserted the ship for the gold fields. She never returned to Sag Harbor and lies under San Francisco landfill.

Some entrepreneurial Blacks earned more money as cooks, barbers, and shopkeepers in the mining camps that they could ever make chasing dreams of gold.

African-Americans made a unique contribution to whaling. Based on the "call and response" of slave spirituals, they composed sea chanteys sung by sailors to the rhythm of their work. It was said that a good song was worth ten men on a rope. Many Black sailors now rest in the century-old cemetery near St. David's AME Zion Church on Route 114. Locked away with them in the holy ground are memories of long voyages where they faced great hardship, but found pride and equality by meeting the challenges of a daunting profession.

✳ ✳ ✳

It Took a Village

Sag Harbor must have presented a fascinating spectacle when the whaling industry peaked in the 1840s. Sailors from all over the globe — white, black, escaped slaves, American Indians, Polynesians, Portuguese — rubbed shoulders with shipyard workers, skilled craftsmen, merchants and shop owners, shipping owners and agents, all engaged in the whaling business. Even the women of the village spun and sewed woolen pea jackets, vests, and shirts for the crews. Horse-drawn carts rumbled along unpaved Main Street carrying tons of supplies to ships about to sail for months or years, while returning vessels unloaded thousands of barrels of oil and thousands of pounds of whalebone.

Over 60 square-rigged whaleships called Sag Harbor their home port. Village yards laid the keels for blunt-bowed vessels that weighed from 250 to 350 tons and cost twenty to sixty thousand dollars. After a battering from the sea, the ships had to be completely refitted before they could sail again. Scores of carpenters, caulkers, riggers, sail and spar makers labored in the yards. Metal workers fixed sheets of copper to the hulls to resist wood-boring worms. Ben Wade's shipyard near today's North Haven Bridge launched the *Sierra Nevada*, reputedly the fastest of the slow-moving breed. In 1796 at a yard in Redwood, Colonel Huntting built a 256-ton whaleship named *Hitty*, after his wife.

The yards also built whaleboats; usually three were carried on the port side of a whaleship, and did the actual pursuing and killing of their quarry. Twenty to twenty-five feet long and relatively light for lowering and lifting, whaleboats could move fast by oar or sail. (One of them is displayed outside the Whaling Museum.) A tub in the whaleboat held 1800 feet of line attached to a harpoon and carefully coiled to avoid kinking when the whale was struck and dove deep to escape.

Years earlier, entrepreneurs from East Hampton and Southampton received a grant to build a wharf that gave townsmen "liberty to pass and repass on said wharf, with their carts and other carriages." Long Wharf expanded in 1808 and 1821 as the whaling industry boomed. Eventually it was sold to the Long Island Railroad that laid tracks onto the pier. Much later, the Town of Southampton and Suffolk County bought the wharf.

Several family-owned shipping firms managed the whaling fleet, among them such prominent names as Huntting, Howell, Dering, French, Mulford and Sleight. James Fenimore Cooper invested in several Sag whalers before he became a famous novelist.

Village blacksmiths, one situated at Bay and Division Streets, hammered out the harpoons and lances for the whaleboats and cutting spades used to strip the blubber from the whale. A vital part of a whaleship was the try works, usually three large iron pots supported on bricks and stanchions above a fire that rendered the blubber. (Several pots sit outside the Whaling Museum.) A pool of water under the fire protected the ship's deck.

To provision the typical whaler putting out to sea, possibly for months or years, local farmers and merchants drove their carts onto Long Wharf with 170 barrels of flour, an equal amount of pork and beef, over a thousand gallons of molasses, 1200 pounds of coffee, 500 pounds of sugar, and hundreds of bushels of beans, corn, apples, peas and potatoes. Coopers along Bay Street delivered water casks and thousands of barrel staves and iron hoops to be assembled on board into barrels to hold oil as whales were killed and rendered. A long, narrow building on Division Street, one of several in the village, housed a ropewalk that twisted miles of hemp fiber for the rigging of the sail-driven whalers.

Clocks and pumps, many made in Sag Harbor, were essential on every vessel. Warehouses storing oil and whalebone were situated on the north end of Main Street. In 1834 Charles Fordham ran a tavern where the Corner Bar is located today. His brother Duke kept a tavern on the opposite corner. S. B. Huntting, Abraham Gardiner, and Josiah Douglas operated general stores. Dotted along Main were Major Hildreth's shoe store, Nelson's lumber yard, Captain Chapman's hat shop, Albert Hedges's livery stable, Seeley's bake shop, and Hunt's office that printed the *Corrector* newspaper.

Farther south from Long Wharf, captains and ship owners built handsome homes. According to the *Guide to Sag Harbor* by Weisburg and Donneson, the Annie Cooper Boyd House on Main —now home of the Historical Society — was at one time the residence of Captain James Hamilton who disappeared while commanding the whaleship *Ocean*. In the yard behind it, the Cooper family built whaleboats, including the one in front of the Whaling Museum. The graceful Hannibal French House next to the Custom House lawn was expanded by the French family, owners of a large whaling company.

Benjamin Huntting from another family built his residence in what is now the museum. Later it was sold to Mrs. Russell Sage for a summer house. Another whaling clan, the Howells, lived for a time in the Napier House on Main across from Palmer Terrace. The Howells erected the Broken Mast Monument in Oakland Cemetery in honor of John who died at 28 while captain of the *France*. The L'Hommedieus who lived in the brick house at the corner of Main and Bayview financed whaling ventures and owned a ropewalk on Glover Street.

Sag Harbor's prosperity from the whaling business faded quickly after 1847. The California Gold rush of 1849 took away many sailors who embarked on several old whaleships to San Francisco and the gold fields. The historic discovery of an oil well in Titusville, Pennsylvania, began the eventual loss of markets for whale oil . Depletion of whale stocks in the South Atlantic required longer, more expensive voyages to the Pacific, raising risks for local investors. Though a few small businesses sprang up, they could not replace the big profits from whaling and Sag Harbor fell into a long period of decline.

Life on a Whaler

We've reported about a few Sag Harbor sailors who jumped ship from whaling vessels and took their chances at life on remote Pacific islands. There weren't many; it was a huge decision to leave home and kin behind. But you can't blame the ones who made such a serious break. Here's how Alexander Laing, a leading marine historian, described life on a whaler:

> It was a hideous business. No free American ever worked and lived in such miserable conditions as the ordinary seaman on a whaler. Even apart from the cramped quarters and wretched food, the whaleman's life — with its long periods of boredom interrupted only by danger — was like a perpetual and grueling war.

Ordinary seamen endured endless voyages in the filth and squalor of the tiny triangular forecastle or "focs'l" in the curving bow of the ship. Rough bunks ran along the hull in a double tier and the only ventilation came from a small hatch overhead that was tightly dogged in bad weather. Men lived in tobacco smoke, smog, and stench for three or four years at a time. Reporter J. Ross Brown wrote about a whaling voyage he made:

> In wet weather when most of the crew was below, cursing, smoking, singing, and spinning yarns, it was a perfect Bedlam. Think of three or four Portuguese, a couple of Irishmen, five or six rough Americans, in a hole about 16 feet wide…so low that a full grown person could not stand upright in it, and so wedged with rubbish as to leave scarcely room for a foothold. It contained 12 small berths, and with sea chests in the tight space around the ladder, seldom admitted of being cleaned. It would seem like exaggeration to say, that I have seen Kentucky pigsties not half so filthy, and in every respect preferable to this miserable hole.

Robert Weir, a crewman on the whaleship *Clara Bell* in 1855, agreed, "We have to work like horses and live like pigs." The ship's specialists had it better than ordinary seamen. Boat steerers, the cooper, and the steward lived in the steerage area, just aft of the mainmast. These quarters were also small, but rarely held more than eight bunks. Officers had the luxury of their own cabins at the stern of the ship. The captain lived in sequestered splendor in a large cabin on the starboard side, equipped with a bed slung on gimbals to compensate for the heeling of the ship. The three mates had small staterooms forward of the captain's quarters.

Everyone on board ate pretty much the same food, and it was awful. It was in the interest of the ship owners to feed the men as cheaply as they could. They finally got the cost down to about 30 cents per man per day — and the food brought constant complaints. Three times a day, the men ate salt beef or salt pork, hard and encrusted after months in a cask. They had to be content with hard tack and, as a treat, duff, a rock-hard concoction of flour, lard and yeast. One

Model of typical whaleship displayed at the Whaling Museum.

whaling sailor described the ritual of dropping bread into hot coffee to soak out the worms.

Historian Laing was writing in general about whaling and whaling crews and we'd like to think that sailors who shipped out on Sag Harbor vessels were treated better and ate better than crews from other ports. Probably not. Maintaining and fitting out ships for long whaling ventures required considerable financing, success wasn't guaranteed, and investors sought reasonable returns for their risks, so it's unlikely Sag Harbor crews were treated any better than sailors from other ports.

Living conditions aboard the whaleships were only the start of challenges. Sailors were still expected to chase and kill the powerful leviathans. When a hunt was successful and a dead whale was towed alongside the ship, the crew cut strips of blubber from the carcass and dropped them through a hatch into a reeking space where other crewmen chopped the blubber into smaller pieces and minced them into more easily rendered "bible-leaves." If more than one whale was killed, the work could go on for a week, the decks covered with great chunks of stinking meat, blood and grease sloshing ankle-deep across the planking. Oil and blood worked into the hair and clothes of the men. The smoke, heat, and sweet-rotten odor of the try-pots created an unworldly scene. The farmstead, mom's cooking, and the rear of a plow horse were certainly more appealing after two or three years on a whaler.

✳ ✳ ✳

His First Whaling Voyage

Call him Joshua. He's been working the family farm just south of Sag Harbor for several years, since he gladly left the one-room colonial schoolhouse. The oldest boy in the family, he just wasn't a student and his brothers were now old enough to help with the endless plowing, planting, fertilizing, harvesting, and feeding pigs and chickens. He finally convinced his mother and father to let him ship out with his cousin Caleb who was first mate on a whaler, and Caleb said he'd look out for him.

The Reverend Henry T. Cheever describes the likely life of a neophyte sailor in *The Whaleman's Adventures* published in New York in 1855. Joshua was strong and hearty and Caleb knew he shouldn't hover over him, he'd have to figure things out on his own, as did the hundreds of lubberly sailors who preceded him. In the first few days after the ship rounded Montauk and headed for the South Atlantic — and maybe the Pacific if they didn't find whales — Caleb had to smile at Joshua's ignorance on deck and in the rigging. The ship's nomenclature is all Greek to Joshua. When ordered to haul the main-brace, he hurries forward and seizes the fore-tack, fore-sheet, or the biggest rope he can find.

If ordered aloft, he creeps up at a snail's pace, constantly looking down, clinging all the time to the shrouds with a tenacity that squeezes the tar out of them. When he reaches the mast top he tries to ascend through the lubber hole as the safer passage. The second mate yells and orders him up through the futtock-shrouds which he slowly accomplishes while perspiration pops out on his forehead. Looking up he sees nothing but bare rope, no place to set his feet. When he reaches the cross-trees, instead of looking for whales he gazes at the deck far below, trying not to think about losing his grip.

Joshua has a young man's big appetite. Or he did. Served on deck in iron-bound wooden kids while the ship bounds over Atlantic swells, after fresh stores have run out the menu might feature greasy pork, hard biscuits and molasses, or salt horse, beans and rice. It may not taste so good at first, but after a few days Joshua gets back his appetite. Later in the voyage, a treat might be donuts fried in whale oil. His eating utensils are a pot, pan, spoon and knife. He must wash and mend his own clothes. His sleep is broken by "Starboard watch, ahoy!" If he is caught napping , he is awakened by a bucket of cold water. When a whale is sighted, the work of cutting and mincing continues around the clock until all the blubber is rendered and casked. When the ship puts into a far-away port in South America or even in the Pacific to take aboard fresh vegetables and possibly recruit new crewmen, Joshua looks forward to adventure in a strange land.

He puts on his most presentable clothes and goes ashore with warnings from cousin Caleb about the potency of local rum and the dangers of local girls. He finds a hospitable tavern a few blocks into town and thinking he is now an experienced sailor, he orders a drink recommended by the kindly bartender. Later he falls senseless in the street, or on the first bench he sees, and recovering hours later finds himself without shoes, money or hat. He returns to the ship with aching head and heavy heart where Caleb is relieved that he has learned a hard lesson without being beaten up. No doubt Reverend Cheever, the author of this fraught tale, often used poor Joshua as an example to impetuous young men who might stray from the farm and the peaceful lanes of Sag Harbor.

Older hands on the whaler would regale young Joshua with tales of disasters that were embellished whenever crews met ashore or while gamming on the high seas. He'd no doubt hear about ships that were attacked by whales, the *Essex* in 1820, the *Pocahontas* in 1850, the *Ann Alexander* in 1851. All three were rammed and sunk by sperm whales after prolonged fights with whaleboats. The *Essex* went down in the Pacific and became famous for the terrible suffering of the crew who were 90 days at sea in open boats and resorted to cannibalism, with only eight of the original crew of 20 surviving.

Many months later when Joshua returned from his first voyage, he probably had greater appreciation for the comforts of home, especially his mother's cooking.

Big Dollars in Whaling

The courageous Sag Harbor ships and crews that voyaged all over the world in search of giant prey have fascinated us with many exciting stories and, I confess, subjects for newspaper columns. But I never gave much thought to the financial side of the business that warranted substantial investments in ships and equipment. Just how much money came from whaling during the "Fruitful Forties" (the 1840s) to pay for the comfortable life styles of many Harborites and the elegant homes that lined Main Street? In a 1957 issue of *Long Island Forum* magazine, I came across an article by local historian Paul Bailey which reports the actual incomes from whaling voyages in those prosperous years.

The figures are impressive. For example, in 1838, whale oil, sperm oil, and whalebone brought in from Sag Harbor ships had a value of $690,000. According to a website which compares figures based on the Consumer Price Index, that's a hefty $17,600,000 in today's dollars. In 1847, at the peak of the business, thirty-two ships arriving at Sag Harbor brought in cargoes worth $995,000, a whopping $29,600,000 in today's money. Sometimes a ship's single voyage brought a profit of thirty percent on its capital investment. The bark *Monmouth* grossed $93,000 on five trips, probably during the 1840s, equivalent to some $3,000,000 today. In 1943, the *Silas Richards*, away for well over two years, brought home a cargo valued at $54,722. That would be $1,810,000 in gross income today.

Historian Bailey puts these dollar amounts in context, pointing out that the average time at sea for those 32 separate arrivals in 1847 was two years and four months. Though the average gross return per ship was slightly over $31,000, this was less than $1,100 per month per ship, hardly a high return on investment. Depletion of whale populations in nearby Atlantic waters required longer voyages into the vast Pacific, even to the Bering Sea, and was one reason for voyages becoming more costly and why investors began showing less interest in financing the expeditions.

Though the whaleship *Plymouth* brought home products that grossed $71,000 ($2,270,000 today), the voyage took them to the North Pacific and stretched three years five months. Furthermore the overhead in the business was considerable, for skilled officers and crews, ship repairs, sails and rigging, miles of rope, dozens of harpoons, lances, spades for cutting in, ship's boats, provisions and myriad other supplies needed aboard a whaler.

The Forum article describes an interesting sidelight to the heady days of whaling. One of the chief worries of the industry as the fleet grew in size was water supply. There was plenty of water but getting it into the ships' tanks was a problem. For some years the only available fresh water came from the Sag Harbor village pump which stood a considerable way up Main Street from the port. Long Wharf was lengthened several times, and it became difficult to find labor to roll empty casks up the street to the pump, work the handle to fill the cask, bung it tightly, then trundle it back to the ship.

In 1827 a few Sag Harbor entrepreneurs formed the Acqueduct Company to supply water directly to the ships. They laid pipes from the well to the end of Long Wharf and pumped the water by means of a windlass operated literally by horse power. Writer Bailey claims that people came from miles away to see this amazing, modern improvement and watch a horse make endless rounds at the outer end of a shaft which kept the well-piston rising and falling.

An even greater improvement came years later when the water company installed an engine to replace the horse, despite complaints about noise from nearby residents, and causing a decline in visitors who liked to watch the horse and stop for refreshment at Fordham's Tavern. The Corner Bar now serves the thirsty at the same location without the attraction of a horse.

In the process of pursuing their arduous trade, sailors in the whaling era set impressive voyaging records. The schooner *Sierra Nevada*, built in Sag Harbor by Benjamin Wade, made the voyage from Shanghai to San Francisco in the world record time of 33 days. The *Washington* circled the globe in 363 days, whaling as she went, without once dropping anchor. She headed south from Sag Harbor through the Atlantic, rounded the Cape of Good Hope, crossed the Indian and Pacific Oceans, weathered Cape Horn, and brought home a full cargo. Wooden ships and iron men.

Offshore Whaling Started the Business

L ong before Sag Harbor built big, square-rigged ships to pursue whales all over the world, the Shinnecock and Montaukett Indians were launching small boats from south shore beaches and hunting the right whales that cruised along the shore in annual migrations. In a lecture in 1998, Noel J. Gish, author and a director of the Suffolk County Historical Society, said that an English explorer saw Indians taking whales along the coast as early as 1620, while Alexander Starbuck in *History of the American Whale Fishery* puts it a little later, in 1644. According to Gish, initially the natives didn't actively hunt as much as they simply awaited whales driven ashore by storm, disease, or accident. They learned to boil the blubber, mix the oil with their corn and beans, or use it as a preservative on animal hides. Once they arrived in Southampton in 1642, the colonists realized the value of the whale and made deals to support the natives' efforts and share in the take. An East Hampton deed in 1648 promised the Indians "to have fynnes and tayles of such whales as shall be cast upp...."

Eventually, a couple of eager braves probably decided that waiting on the beach was non-productive and boring, and launched dugout canoes into the surf to attack the whales offshore. At first they used wooden spears and developed methods for attaching drogues to tire out wounded whales until they succumbed and could be towed to shore. Local blacksmiths forged improved whaling tools, and sturdier boats were stationed along the beaches ready for the cry of "whale off." Once dragged to the beach, the whale was cut into, its blubber rendered in huge try pots, its baleen and up to 700 pounds of bone extracted. The whale men ignored complaints from Southampton residents about the stink of boiling blubber. Recipes at the time included mince pies made with whale meat. Whale oil lamps and candles were highly prized, and the oil could be used to protect farm tools from rust. Bones became buttons and corset stays, baleen became chair springs, hair brushes, and even buggy whips.

By 1680, Amagansett was the most profitable village for shore whaling and by 1687 seven companies were in business along the south shore. Frederick Schmitt in *Mark Well the Whale* wrote that in 1700 a woman walking from East Hampton to Bridgehampton counted 13 stranded animals and countless others spouting near shore.

Where there are profits, taxes surely follow, and Robert Hunter, Royal Governor of New York, passed a tax on whale oil and bone. The move angered 70-year-old Samuel Mulford so he sailed to London to protest, eventually gaining an audience with King George I who repealed the tax a year later. Mulford earned some notoriety, reports Gish, when he foiled London's pickpockets by lining his pockets with fishhooks, catching thieves in the act.

According to *Whale Off* by Edwards and Rattray, Hamptons beaches produced 2,148 barrels of oil in 1687. By 1707, as larger sloops began venturing out for two or three weeks, the yield grew to 4,000 barrels. *Whale Off* describes a six-man crew made up of a multi-tasking boatsteerer-harpooner who pulled an oar, threw the harpoon, then tended the towline, a bow-oarsman who secured the sail and mast when a whale was struck, a midship-oarsman, a tub-oarsman who carefully coiled 100-fathoms of rope into a tub to avoid snags, a stroke who helped haul in the towline and called the beat to the oarsmen, and the boat-header/captain who steered and went forward at the critical time to kill the whale with a lance. The boat carried two harpoons, two lances, and a cutting-in spade. Thole pins that held the oars were quieted with padding to avoid alarming the quarry.

Inevitably, the number of whales lolling close to shore dwindled and it was necessary to pursue the leviathans farther at sea. Sag Harbor on the inside of the south fork with its large, well-protected port could accommodate and supply big, ocean-able ships, and its fame as a major whaling center began to grow. Many of the same natives who had hunted whales along the shore were sought as experienced crew for the long, dangerous voyages that took them to the far reaches of the oceans. But occasional shore whaling continued and as late as December of 1893, the *New York Tribune* reported that two Southampton boats commanded by Captains Rogers and White killed a large right whale. Estimated value: $2,000. ($50,000 in today's dollars.)

❋ ❋ ❋

Tough Boats for Tough Business

Big, square-rigged sailing ships took whaling crews to the far corners of the oceans, but it was the small boats they carried aboard that met in face-to-jaws battle with the leviathans, and often got wacked by their huge fins and tails. Sag Harbor's whaleships sailed with five or six of these rugged little boats, most built in the village by William Henry Cooper. According to Cooper family papers at the Long Island Museum in Stony Brook, William turned out 747 whaleboats during the heyday of the industry in the first half of the 19th century, along with 110 bunker boats and 63 craft for other jobs. The Sag Harbor Whaling Museum displays a Cooper-built whaleboat from the ship *Concordia* measuring 25 feet long and 74 inches in the beam. Cooper also repaired damaged boats but, given the abuse they suffered during years' long voyages, whaleboats were considered disposable.

The Cooper clan is all over East End history and all the men seemed to be named William. Barbara Schwartz of the Sag Harbor Historical Society says boat builder William Henry Cooper was the son of Caleb, grandson of Thomas, and great grandson of John, one of the founders of Southampton. William Henry had a son born in 1817 who was always referred to as William H. or William Huntting. William Huntting Cooper was the name handed down to all the next generations. We hesitate to delve any further into the Cooper family tree.

The *Concordia* whaleboat has a mast step but no keel or center-board so it probably sailed downwind whenever possible. Otherwise five rowers propelled the craft while the helmsman manned a long steering oar. A heavy round "loggerhead" at the bow controlled hundreds of feet of hemp line attached to a harpoon. Once pierced, the giant quarry often took its tormenters on a "Nantucket sleigh-ride," towing the whaleboat and its crew. Whaleboat design began well over a thousand years ago when Inuit hunters developed skin-hulled boats to pursue migratory whales that fed close to the northwest coast of North America. Except for different materials, whaleboat designs haven't changed all that much.

James Fenimore, another Cooper from a different branch of the family and half-owner of the whaleship *Union*, described whaleboats in an early novel:

> It is sharp at both ends, in order that it may back off, as well as pull on, it steers with an oar, instead of with a rudder, in order that the bow may be thrown around to avoid danger when not in motion; it is buoyant, and made to withstand the shock of waves at both ends; and it is light and shallow, though strong, that it may be pulled with facility. When it is remembered that one of these little egg-shells…is often dragged through troubled waters at the rate of ten or twelve knots…one can easily understand how much depends on the form, buoyancy and strength. Among seaman, it is commonly thought that a whaleboat is the safest craft of the sort in which men can trust themselves in rough water.

Documents in the Cooper collection record that William Henry bought large quantities of cedar planks, but also oak and smaller amounts of pine, ash, and birch. If natural curved oak wasn't available, Cooper steam-bent the ribs, stems and stern pieces for his boats. One

A typical whaleboat sits outside the Whaling Museum.

document shows William Cooper's cost of whaleboat production to be $33.66, "exclusive of overhead." Author Francis Turano describes Cooper's business in a recent issue of the *Long Island Historical*

Journal which is available online. With the help of two journeymen and two apprentices, William Henry Cooper could build 70 whale-boats in a year at a boat shop next to Long Wharf and another at 168 Main Street. The Long Wharf shop was destroyed in 1845 in one of the massive fires that periodically swept Sag Harbor. The Historical Society recently completed a small whaleboat shop behind the Annie Cooper Boyd House which holds some of William Henry Cooper's tools and facsimiles of his business transactions.

When the whaling business dropped off after 1850, William Henry and his brother Gilbert opened a Main Street store selling dry goods, groceries, and hardware, while continuing as whaling agents for a dwindling number of voyages. Between 1820 and 1859, William Henry owned shares in over 50 whaling voyages probably through the Long Island Whaling Company which, added to boat building, may account for Cooper's prosperity. In 1852, he calculated his assets at $51,642. Adjusted for 2016 dollars, this translates into $1,614,125, making William Henry Cooper a substantial member of the Sag Harbor community. In 1843, only a prosperous Harborite could have ordered from New York City a "swell-front, grand action pianoforte, made of mahogany."

Whaling at Age 16

In a spurt of graphic prose, Erastus Denison Bill, aboard the Sag Harbor ship *Citizen*, described chasing a whale in the North Pacific. "We are in the lead when the whale comes up to blow. The Captain expectorating freely regardless of the wind, bends forward to press upon my oar and exclaims earnestly, 'Spring my men. Spring hard.' The pupils of his eyes expand and dilate, making them look like blazing stars, and at the same time his jaws work as the tobacco juice continues to fly." His florid description of Captain David Lansing was unusual since Bill normally wrote spare descriptions of his life at sea. Perhaps he added drama later.

As a boy with a widowed mother, poor family fortune, and scant schooling, Erastus worked summers on a farm in exchange for food and clothing. In 1843 he shipped out as an apprentice seaman on a voyage that exposed him to angry whales, death and maiming, floggings and mutiny, thousands of miles from home. Mulford and Sleight, the ship's agents, advanced him 50 dollars so he could equip himself for the voyage. At sea only a few days he nearly fell from the top of the main mast and later trembled at the memory.

Citizen sails southeast in the Atlantic around Africa's Cape of Good Hope into the Indian Ocean, then to Van Diemen's Land (now Tasmania) and New Zealand, encountering vicious storms, their first whales, and occasionally touching ashore to replenish food supplies. Third officer Michael Arch dies of "an intestinal disorder," is sewn into a canvass shroud weighted with bricks and buried at sea. The crew enjoys idyllic time in the Sandwich (Hawaiian) Islands. Assigned as an oarsman in the Captain's boat, Erastus one day is replaced by Isaac Post, the ship's cooper, who is killed when a whale smashes the boat with its powerful tail. On Bonin Island south of Japan they meet another Sag Harbor ship, *Manhattan*, captained by Mercator Cooper.

In Northern Pacific whaling grounds during summer 1844, Erastus claimed "there are more than five hundred ships cruising over these grounds and more than one thousand men killed...." which could be an old salt's exaggeration. On Raratonga, when the Captain announces they might remain at sea for another whaling season, some of the crew plot mutiny but the officers seize the ringleaders and put them in irons. The ship heads for home anyway and reaches Sag Harbor in July 1846.

Erastus Bill's "200th lay [share of the profits] amounts to the fifty dollar advance for my outfit...."

With no jobs ashore, Erastus ships out again from Sag Harbor as a harpooner, "As I near the wharf, the street fills…. People go in and out of places where the clink of glasses and the shuffling of feet keep time to the squeak and throb of the violin." The second voyage departs September 19, 1846, headed for the tip of South America. On October 14th the steward, "being sulky and unruly, is seized up in the mizzen rigging and flogged, put in irons…."

Erastus harpoons his first whale off Patagonia. The beast runs off until finally "the Captain's lance now pierces the whale's vitals." The whale yields 80 barrels of oil worth $3,000. Four of the crew desert on the Sandwich Islands but are caught and flogged. On July 6th Erastus harpoons a 100-barrel whale and the Captain yells, "that boy has killed that whale." A few days later while rendering blubber a crewman falls into the "deck pot" and gets "scalded and greased." When a whale breaks harpooner John Babcock's leg, they steer for San Francisco to seek medical help. They meet him months later, on crutches, his leg gone. News comes of gold in California and the Captain allows the first officer and six native crewmen to leave the ship. *Citizen* enters New York Harbor on February 1, 1849, docking at Pier 12 on the East River. This time Bill's lay amounts to $625, worth approximately $17,000 in today's currency.

Erastus eventually moved to Illinois where he raised a large family and farmed for 40 years. Perhaps he felt like the old sailor who, looking for a place to retire, said he would carry an oar over his shoulder and walk inland until someone asked, "What's that?" In March, 1905 the *Sag Harbor Express* printed Bill's original journals. His grandson Robert Wesley Bill assembled them in a book titled *Citizen* (available at the Historical Society's Annie Cooper Boyd house). Erastus Denison Bill died on December 23, 1905.

Whale or Hippo?

When they rowed ashore in a ship's boat on the east coast of Africa to look for firewood and provisions, the sailors of the Sag Harbor whaling ship thought they spotted a whale in shoal water. Suddenly they hit something underwater. Crewman Charles Nordhoff wrote, in somewhat dated literary style,

> As we backed off, an enormous beast slowly raised its head above the water, gave a loud snort, and dove down again.... "Whatever it is," said the mate, whose whaling blood was up, "if it comes within reach of my iron, I'll make fast to it, lads — so pull ahead. Pull easy, lads, I see him…there's his back.... Stern all!" shouted the mate as he darted his iron into a back as broad as a small sperm whale's. The infuriated beast made desperate lunges in every direction, making the white water fly. We could now see the whole shape of the creature, as, in his agony and surprise, he raised himself high above the surface. We all recognized at once the Hippopotamus, as he is represented in books of natural history.

Nordhoff continued telling his East African adventure in his book *Whaling and Fishing* which was published in 1855. "Giving a savage roar, (the hippopotamus) bent his head around until he grasped the shank of the iron between his teeth. With one jerk he drew it out of his bleeding quarter, and shaking it violently, dove down to the bottom." When the beast rose up again the mate killed him by planting a lance deep into his heart. The sailors towed the body ashore and measured it at 15-feet long from head to tiny tail. Natives told the sailors that the hippo was good eating so they cut off a large portion of the fore quarter and shared it with the natives before going back on board and enjoying a hippo steak feast. Today we would rightfully protect the animals, but in those long ago times, fresh meat was a delicacy to the whalers.

In another part of his book, Nordhoff told about competing for a dead whale with sharks that gathered while the crew stripped blubber from the carcass. He describes the gruesome work on a whaler.

An immense number of sharks had gathered around the ship, attracted thither by the blood and scent of our prize. As far as the eye could distinguish them, their dorsal fins could be seen gliding over the water, all hurrying to the scene of slaughter, eager to secure a share of the prize. The extraordinary number of these sea lawyers present was equaled only by their rapacity.

Before we began cutting in, they had already commenced their meal. Taking advantage of a heave of the swell, a shark would wriggle up on top of the whale, and setting his wide open mouth against the solid blubber, would bite out a piece.... The officers spent their leisure moments in cutting at them with the spades, and one man was stationed abreast of the whale's head, with a long sharp spade, to keep them off that part.

I saw one cut in such a manner that his entrails protruded into the water, and yet this animal, which it was to be supposed would almost immediately die, wriggled itself up on the whale, and took out a huge mouthful, paying for its temerity by having the greater part of its tail cut off.

"It is almost impossible to kill a shark..." wrote Nordhoff.

The amount of suffering they will undergo before death ensues, is really marvelous. I have seen all entrails taken out of one, and yet after lying about on deck for an hour, he bit and crushed a stout ash pole between his teeth.... There are few instances on record of a shark having bitten a man while cutting in. There is too great a superabundance of other food....

> I have seen a man working on the whale, with a shark close beside him: he simply giving the fish a kick with his heavy sea-boot, when he became aware of its close proximity.

Charles Nordhoff had shipped aboard the Sag Harbor whaler sometime in the mid-19th century when it stopped at New Bedford to fill out its crew. Nordhoff was a journalist before serving for three years in the U.S. Navy. After his service he took various jobs at sea before returning to journalism. From 1853 to 1857 he worked for various newspapers, finally spending ten years on the *New York Evening Post*. He was the grandfather of Charles Bernard Nordhoff, co-author of *Mutiny on the Bounty*. Obviously writing talent ran in the family.

Petticoat Whalers of Sag Harbor

Whaling was tough on Sag Harbor wives who stayed at home, often tending many kids and perhaps a farm to take care of, while their husbands were gone for years to remote corners of the world. But there were quite a few Sag Harbor women who didn't stay home, they sailed with their spouses, sometimes bringing the children, and endured the dangers, boredom, and loneliness that came with chasing whales. They may have been America's earliest feminists.

Emeline Winters, born in 1819 to Sydney and Cynthia Hallock, married Captain Jonas Winters when she was 19 years old, and regularly sailed with him aboard the whaler *Elizabeth Frith*. Years later when a voyage reached the Sandwich (now Hawaiian) Islands she gave birth in Honolulu to a second baby. In 1852, she had remained in Sag Harbor, but eager to see the captain as he headed home from his long whaling cruise, she took her two children, Clarence and Adia, probably hitching a ride on an outgoing whaler, to join him on St.

Helena Island in the southeast Atlantic Ocean. Joan Druett, in *The Sailing Circle*, told about Emeline along with a score of other adventurous Sag Harbor wives.

Unlike merchant vessels that tried to keep to a schedule, whaleships were seldom in a hurry since they usually cruised back and forth searching a large patch of ocean. So when another whaleship was sighted, especially if its home port was Sag Harbor, or Greenport, or Orient, and there were wives on both ships, great excitement ensued at the prospect of a gam. The ships would heave to, a boat from one of them would be lowered and the wife and captain rowed across to meet the other wife and captain.

Gams were an opportunity to catch up on whaling gossip and news from home. No wonder the women were starved for news and companionship — Carolyn Lowen sailed from Sag Harbor with her husband, Captain James Madison Tabor, for a honeymoon cruise on the whaleship *Augusta* in July, 1857, and didn't arrive back home until January, 1861.

A whaleship was really no place for a lady. The quarters were cramped, the company rough, and the trade gruesome and dangerous. The ships rolled easily and most wives got terribly seasick. They lived a solitary kind of existence, surrounded by men, forced to pass the time, perhaps for years, while they waited for the ship to fill up with oil.

In 1857 when Mrs. William James Grant of Cold Spring Harbor and Mrs. Eliza Edwards of the *Black Eagle* out of Sag Harbor waited in Honolulu for their husbands to return from the northern whaling season, they felt lucky to have each other and also to be boarding at a house kept by Mrs. Cartwright, wife of a Shelter Island man. Elizabeth Chapman Green of Southampton who sailed with her husband James on the *Nimrod* in 1851, stayed in Lahaina, Maui, with Mrs. Thomas Long of New London. In September 1847 Elizabeth's sister-in-law Maria, wife of Captain Barney Green of the Sag Harbor whaleship

Ontario shopped the stores of Honolulu with Mary Brewster of Stonington.

Martha Brown sailed with her husband Captain Edwin Peter Brown on the *Lucy Ann* of Greenport on August 21, 1847 when she was 26 years old, leaving her two-year-old daughter Ella with relatives. Four days later they met the whaleship *Roanoke* also outbound from Greenport and sailed together to Fayal in the Azores. Master of the *Roanoke* was Captain Smith Baldwin of Shelter Island who was accompanied by his 23-year-old bride Maria Cartwright Baldwin. Maria handled the ship so well that she could take the helm even while tacking. Her first child was born at St. Helena. To give an idea of its remoteness, St. Helena is in the middle of the South Atlantic, 1200 miles from the African coast and 1800 miles from South America.

Sarah Eliza Jennings of Sag Harbor was aboard the *Mary Gardiner* in 1861 when a Confederate raider chased the ship for two hours. Her husband Captain Andrew Jennings was so elated at his escape that he gave up whaling and took up blockade running. The *Mary Gardiner* must have been faster than most whaleships which were fat and blunt-bowed, built not for speed but for hauling barrels of oil.

According to author Joan Druett, most captains and wives occupied a cramped cabin in the far stern of the ship with a tiny sitting room crammed with heavy furniture, a chart table, and chair. Meals were eaten at a massive table in the forward cabin and shared with three or four mates, "who were often not very cultivated fellows."

Renowned for her cultured manners and beauty before her marriage to Captain Jetur Rose, Caroline Rose, who was raised in Water Mill, managed to tutor her daughter Emma on the ship despite the disapproval of missionaries in Hawaii who said "no one on a whaler ever knew anything." We wonder what she thought when one of the crew stepped up to complain about the quality of the food and threw a cask of butter overboard to dramatize his point. Captain Rose picked up the complainer and tossed him overboard after the butter.

2

Native Americans and Colonial Life

Algonquins Enjoyed the Hamptons

Before there was Sag Harbor, before the Hamptons even existed, the Woodland Indians of the Algonquian Nation enjoyed a relatively peaceful life on the East End of Long Island. The local Indians got along well together and spent their time hunting, fishing, planting crops, and raising families. Several hundred years before the "beautiful people" discovered the Hamptons, beautiful people were already living here, and they didn't have to fight traffic on weekends.

Italian explorer Giovanni Verrazzano described the natives he met:

> The people excel us in size; they are of bronze color, some inclining more to whiteness, others to tawny color; the face sharply cut, the hair long and black, upon which they bestow the greatest study in adorning it; the eyes black and alert, the bearing kind and gentle.

They dressed modestly, not in bikinis or Speedos. The men wore breech cloths of deerskin front and rear, and in winter, robes of deer hide or animal fur. The women wore skirts and tops of deer skin while both braves and squaws wore skin moccasins, leggings, and a belt.

One historian, William Golder, wrote that Indians lived in wigwams constructed by digging a circular trench two or three feet deep and 15 feet in diameter. They drove saplings into the trench and lashed the tops together to create a framework on which they laid grass mats. A hole in the dome let out smoke from a cooking and heating fire. A replica of one of these dwellings sits outside the Shinnecock Museum on Route 27A, a little east of Southampton College.

The women cultivated corn, beans and squash, prepared meals and clothing, and wove fish traps and nets while the men hunted and fished and chased the occasional whale that appeared offshore (today's husbands would love a deal like that).

They also ground chestnuts and acorns to make flat bread. Meat sources abounded — raccoon, opossum, fox, squirrel, groundhog, rabbit, beaver, muskrat, and, most importantly, deer. John Strong, a professor of history at Southampton College who has written extensively about the East End Indians, says that the natives here usually prepared communal meals in a large stew pot made from clay. And long before today's sophisticated chefs discovered the technique, the Indians baked fish, fowl and small game in clay crocks to retain the juices and flavor. Clams, oysters, mussels, and scallops were plentiful, and long before it became a special summer event, the Algonquians baked clams in pits heated with red hot stones and covered with eel grass.

Cynics probably think wampum was invented by Paramount Studios, but it actually was an important art and craft. The Algonquians had a ready supply of hard clam shells, especially quahogs, which the women (in their spare time?) laboriously fashioned into wampum beads using crude stone and bone tools. Wampum adorned necklaces, bracelets and decorations for clothes and moccasins, and was assembled into bands and belts which conveyed messages to other Indians and later were a form of exchange with Europeans.

Colonists from Massachusetts arrived in North Sea Harbor in Southampton in 1640, seeking to establish a village, procure land, and plant crops. The local Indians were friendly and helped the settlers survive their early difficult years. But a critical confusion involving land ownership eventually arose. To the Indians, says John Strong, land was part of nature to be used by all the people and it made no sense to divide it into privately owned acreage. Europeans considered land a commodity that could be bought and sold, as we do today. Indians considered goods and gifts from colonists as gestures of friendship for simply sharing access, not as payment for land. This cultural discord inevitably led to disputes when the Europeans claimed property ownership and wanted to keep it for their own use.

Strong notes that popular history generally lists 13 tribes on Long Island, as if these were formal sub-tribes within the Algonquian Nation. Initially, there were no such official entities, the Indians more likely identifying themselves with clans or communities. After 1650 a tribal system emerged among the Montauketts, Shinnecocks, and other groups as a means of survival against encroaching English settlers. (Even today, hundreds of years later, stresses continue. At this writing, the Shinnecocks are pressing Southampton for protection of newly discovered burial sites which might be found on private properties.)

Place names grew into tribal names. The Montauketts, living in the area from Bridgehampton to what became Montauk Point and Gardiner's Island, took the Algonquin word for "a fortified place;" the Shinnecocks adopted the word for "at the level land" covering Eastport to Bridgehampton; the Manhasets' name means "island sheltered by islands" from their home on Shelter Island; and the Corchaugs, dwelling from Wading River to Orient, used the Algonquian term for "principal place." Their numbers were surprisingly small. Several sources say there were perhaps 6,500 Indians on all of Long Island in the mid-17th century with 500 more or less in each tribe.

A chief or sachem headed each of the small tribes, mainly through respect and persuasion, exerting power only when necessary. Like a chairman of the board, the chief of the Montauketts, Wyandanch, was grand sachem of the East End Indians, and the primary contact with English colonists. He was regularly criticized as being too accommodating. Though the Algonquians on the East End were peaceful people, they were forced to defend themselves against aggressive clans from Connecticut and Rhode Island. Ninigret, sachem of the Rhode Island Niantics, was a constant threat and in one episode raided the Montauketts, kidnapping Wyandanch's daughter, supposedly on her wedding day. Wyandanch asked for help from the English, and Lion Gardiner came to his aid.

NEAR THIS SPOT
IN JUNE 1640
LANDED THE COLONISTS FROM LYNN. MASS
WHO FOUNDED SOUTHAMPTON
THE FIRST ENGLISH SETTLEMENT
IN THE STATE OF NEW YORK

Colonists landed at Conscience Point near North Sea harbor.

To learn more about the lives of the East End Indians and see some of their handicrafts, visit the Shinnecock Museum in Southampton or the Southold Indian Museum on the North Fork.

The Shinnecocks Continue to Endure

People keep predicting the end of the Shinnecocks. Headlines like "The Last of the Shinnecocks" have appeared for years over stories about the death of another elderly tribal member. Some newspapers traced the tribe's demise all the way back to an incident in December,1876 when the cargo ship *Circassian* grounded off Southampton. The call went out for a salvage crew to rescue the ship, and eleven Shinnecock men volunteered to board the vessel. But the *Circassian* broke apart, casting crew and Shinnecocks into the freezing water. No one survived.

In 1936, the *Long Island Press* asserted, "They were the last of the pure-blooded male Indians on the Island," as though no one else was living on the reservation at the time. The same story cropped up earlier in the *Brooklyn Eagle*. Nineteenth century "scholars" saw another reason for the tribe's impending demise, claiming that inter-marriages between Indians and whites and blacks doomed the race to extinction. Today's tribal members state emphatically, "We're still here!"

The original English settlers in the mid-17th century on the East End of Long Island held the attitude that Indian culture was inferior to their own, justifying their acquisition of Indian lands by fair means or foul. In our "enlightened" 21st century, remnants of that attitude seem to linger which naturally angers the tribe's descendants as they make claims for restitution of what they believe was unfairly taken from them.

The tribe keeps state, county, and local governments on edge — among other things by pursuing the right to establish a gambling casino somewhere on Long Island, by pressing a lawsuit launched in 2005 seeking to reclaim 3,600 acres of prime Southampton real estate worth billions of dollars, and by demanding a Southampton regulation to respect Indian burial sites, even on private property.

The Shinnecocks were a small part of the great Algonquian Nation that was spread all over the Northeastern United States. Historian

John Strong says that Native Americans in the early 17th century more likely identified themselves with a local clan or matriarchy. Tribal allegiance, he suggests, developed later when the Indians realized they should band together to resist encroachment by English settlers.

The Shinnecocks occupied the land along the South Fork between the Unquachaug tribe to the west and the Montauketts to the east. When the white men first arrived at Conscience Point in Southampton in 1640 Nowedonah was chief of the Shinnecocks. He was a brother of Wyandanch, chief of the Montauketts who later became grand sachem of the East End tribes.

Soon after, he agreed to "sell" eight square miles of land to the English for sixteen winter coats and sixty bushels of corn. The Indians considered such a transaction an agreement to share the land rather than to transfer ownership. Francis Jennings, director of the Center for the History of the American Indian, stated that when the Native Americans lost their land, for whatever reason, they also lost political power. "Property and liberty were synonymous in the 17th and 18th centuries. When an Indian was dispossessed of his land, he lost all hope of finding any niche in the society called 'civilized' except that of a servant or slave."

Like other Algonquians on the East End, the Shinnecocks hunted game, gathered abundant seafood from bay and ocean, and were renowned for fabricating valuable wampum from thick quahog shells they could pick up along the shore. Farming apparently was not extensive among Native Americans in the region because, according to Quaker settlers, "the land requires manure to make it produce well, and few have the money to purchase it." And of course there were many other means of sustenance.

Before long, coastal whaling became an important source of revenue which, says John Strong, the Shinnecocks shared with the settlers who provided them with 23-ft cedar boats equipped with iron lances and harpoons. When a whale was sighted offshore, two boats, each holding four oarsmen, a harpooner, and a steersman, were launched and worked together to kill the leviathan and tow it to shore. There the crews rendered the blubber and cleaned the bones, a hard job of several smelly days. The experience gained from coastal whaling made Shinnecock sailors ideal recruits for ships venturing out of Sag Harbor. The character of Tashtego in Herman Melville's *Moby Dick* was drawn from the hundreds of Algonquians who manned whaleships and chased their huge prey throughout the oceans during the 19th century.

The Shinnecock tribe is already recognized by the State of New York, and its reservation of 750 acres where some 150 members still live is self governing. More members of the tribe reside elsewhere on Long Island. Federal recognition of the tribe was granted in 2010. Trustee Larry Gumbs said that once the tribe achieved official recognition it would move quickly to build a casino on Long Island, but that has yet to happen. Whatever the outcome, the Shinnecocks have a history of carrying on against all odds.

In his book *Native New Yorkers*, Evan Pritchard tells a story that reflects the character of the Shinnecocks. When World War II began, the tribe objected to the draft, saying it was a sovereign nation within New York State and not beholden to the United States Federal Government. As soon as the Shinnecocks won recognition of their position and were under no obligation to fight, most of the eligible males signed up and served honorably in the armed forces. Independent, persevering, indefatigable, the Shinnecock tribe continues to endure.

Wyandanch Led East End Indians through Time of Violent Change

The trials and tribulations of Wyandanch, Grand Sachem of the Algonquians on the East End of Long Island, would have made a perfect Shakespearean tragedy. The Indian chief had to cope with a dangerous and shifting political scene in the middle of the 17th century. He worked to keep peace between his own people and encroaching English settlers, both dissatisfied with his efforts. He had to defend his tribe against marauding natives from Connecticut and Rhode Island, his own daughter kidnapped in one of the raids. He felt powerless to halt the destruction of traditional Indian culture and saw his people decimated by European diseases. He himself succumbed to plague in 1659, though some historians think he was poisoned. Poison would have been a classical end to the saga of this beleaguered leader.

The Indians on the East End lived fairly well, enjoying the riches of sea and land, until they were sucked into a conflict involving the English, Dutch, and aggressive New England sachems. In 1637 English soldiers massacred the Pequots in Connecticut who had been killing colonists and were exacting tribute from neighboring tribes, including those on Long Island. Realizing that Ninigret, the aggressive sachem of the Niantics, would attempt to fill the void left by the Pequots, and seeing that resistance to the English was futile, the young Montaukett sachem Wyandanch negotiated a pact with 38-year old Lion Gardiner, an English military commander.

The resentful Ninigret became a lifelong enemy and developed an obsession to dominate Wyandanch and cut his ties with his European allies, telling him "the English will speak much but do little." John A. Strong's definitive history *The Montaukett Indians of Eastern Long Island* recounts Ninigret's raid on the East End in 1638 when he stripped and humiliated Wyandanch and seized thirty fathoms of wampum. This would be a theft of 180 feet of bands of the beads and discs laboriously fabricated from thick shells. Wyandanch appealed to Roger Ludlow, deputy governor of Connecticut who forced Ninigret to make restitution.

Realizing this wouldn't be the end of the feud, Wyandanch invited Lion Gardiner to buy land adjacent to the Montauketts, which the English were happy to do if only to keep out the Dutch. In 1639 Gardiner bought the large island between the two forks which bears his name, though he initially called it the Isle of Wight. Over the years the two became close friends. Recognizing his influence, the East End Indians accepted Wyandanch as their grand sachem. In 1644 he and other chiefs from the region met with English commissioners and granted them "exclusive purchase rights to eastern Long Island." They also agreed that any Indian committing a crime against the English would be turned over to the English for justice. To further stymie the Dutch the English purchased 31,000 acres from the tribes between Southampton and Napeague Bay.

Native Americans initially considered such deals merely agreements to share use of the land, not as surrender of ownership. Strong points out that the Indians gradually were drawn into the web of an economic and political system where they had less control over their own affairs. Access to European manufactured products eventually made them dependent on goods they couldn't produce themselves and put them into debt to the English.

The sachems' judicial arrangement with the English was severely tested a few years later when Southampton settlers accused some Shinnecocks of murdering an English woman. The Shinnecocks refused an investigation, offering only to pay retribution to the family. Gardiner asked Wyandanch to intervene with the Shinnecocks and he was able to secure consent to seize the braves responsible and take them to Hartford for trial. They were found guilty and hanged. Later Wyandanch was called on to settle a boundary dispute between the Shinnecocks and Southampton.

Ninigret again attacked, killing thirty Montauketts and kidnapping Wyandanch's daughter Quashawam. Lion Gardiner raised money for her ransom. When Ninigret continued to demand tribute from the Montauketts, the English supplied ammunition to Wyandanch which he used in an ambush of Niantics who had paddled to Block Island. The Montauketts killed Ninigret's nephew, two Niantic sachems and 60 of their braves, a victory which boosted Wyandanch's standing with the English and his own people. He became an important intermediary with the settlers, settling problems on land use, Indian hunting of free-range English hogs, destruction of Indian crops by English cattle, and reducing the punishment of Shinnecocks who had plotted arson in Southampton. When the unrelenting Ninigret continued to threaten, the English hired John Young of Southold to blockade Long Island Sound against invading canoes.

Wyandanch sold a stretch of beach land west of Southampton to Lion Gardiner with an agreement that the Montauketts could take the tails and fins of whales cast up on the beach and sell the baleen and oil to the English. Later when two East Hampton men borrowed Wyandanch's canoe to carry supplies to Gardiner's Island but neglected to tie it up securely, Wyandanch sued for damages and was awarded ten shillings. During the last years of his life he supervised nearly all land sales as far west as Hempstead, realizing the Indians were powerless to resist the settlements.

The grand sachem died sometime in 1659, by poisoning claimed Lion Gardiner, but more likely from a plague that killed two-thirds of the Algonquians on Long Island between 1659 and 1664. Gardiner lamented, "My friend and brother is gone." The Europeans induced Wyandanch's widow to "sell" more land and soon completely dominated the Native Americans.

One sachem made the poignant comment, "They take our land away every day, a little and a little." Eventually the discouraged Montaukett tribe moved to upper New York State and Algonquian life on the East End neared an end. The political struggle continues even today as the Shinnecocks strive to bolster their tribal standing and seek casino rights and relief from tax laws.

✳ ✳ ✳

Lion Gardiner Kept Peace on the East End

"It was not a squeamish age," said a historian describing Lion Gardiner's parley with Wyandanch, a leader of the Montauk tribe and an influential Native American for much of Long Island. Gardiner demanded "If you kill all the Pequots that come to you, and send me their heads, then you shall have trade with us.... If you have any Indians that have killed English, you must bring me their heads also...." Despite this potentially gory beginning, Gardiner and Wyandanch became close allies, even friends, and between them kept the peace on the east end of Long Island.

Most of us know little about Gardiner's Island, sitting between the north and south forks, nor of the man who gave it his name. Initially Gardiner called it the Isle of Wight, since its shape reminded him of that island off the south coast of England. A soldier, Gardiner arrived in the new world in 1635 with the commission to establish a fort in Saybrook at the mouth of the Connecticut River to protect an expected colony of settlers. In the fall 1989 issue of the *Long Island Historical Journal* Professor Roger Wunderlich of the University at Stony Brook wrote that Gardiner was probably a gentleman without title, ranking below the nobility, and may have taken the Saybrook job for the one-hundred pounds per year it paid.

Gardiner dreaded the Pequots, an aggressive Native American tribe in Connecticut that battled constantly with colonists and other Indians. In one attack on the fort, a Pequot arrow pierced Gardiner's leg. Finally a large force of colonists and Indian allies exacted heavy casualties on the Pequots which quieted them down for a while. But knowing there could still be trouble ahead, Wyandanch canoed over the sound to Saybrook and made his deal with Gardiner in exchange for protection. The pact relieved eastern Long Island of the English–Indian warfare that plagued New England for forty years. During their stay in Saybrook, Gardiner and his wife Mary had a son, David, and daughter, Mary.

Other tribes prodded Wyandanch to turn against the English, but he had complete confidence in Gardiner. When the Saybrook settlement petered out, Gardiner bought his island a few miles off East Hampton for "ten coates of trading cloath." Soon after, he received a confirming grant from the King's grantee for Long Island, thus becoming "independent of every other settlement, and subordinate only to the general government of the Colony."

Gardiner's Island is substantial, seven-and-a-half miles long and three miles across at its widest point. In 1798 a family descendant described its soil as good for wheat, its timber mostly of large white oak, with brooks, springs, and ponds keeping it watered. Though Gardiner and Wyandanch were able to preserve the peace, other Indian tribes continued fighting. According to Curtiss Gardiner, in 1654 the Narragansetts from Rhode Island swooped down on the Montauks the night before Wyandanch's daughter was to be wed, killed the groom and kidnapped the bride. Mostly through Gardiner's efforts, ransom was raised and the daughter returned safely to her distraught father. A grateful Wyandanch gave Lion Gardiner land between Huntington and Setauket, citing Gardiner's "kindness, counsel and advice in our prosperity."

When Wyandanch was ordered to come to Southampton to testify in a murder case involving Indians, his people feared for his safety, but Gardiner quieted their concerns by presenting himself at the Montauk camp, declaring he would stay until "you all know it is well with your sachem." Lion Gardiner died at 64, and in 1686 Governor Thomas Dongan granted his son David a new patent and the new name for the island. In modern times the heirs have struggled with rising maintenance costs and taxes.

Gardiner's Island is now in the hands of Alexandra Creel Goelet, a seventeenth-generation direct descendant. She established family trusts to own the island and entered a conservation easement with East Hampton that stipulates the town will not rezone, change the assessment, or acquire the island by condemnation through 2025.

Historian Wunderlich admired Lion Gardiner for learning the native language and gaining the trust of his Indian neighbors, "treating them without condescension." His and Wyandanch's diplomacy headed off interracial warfare. Gardiner and his wife, says the historian, are symbols of the transition first generation immigrants made from the old world to the new. "They were Americans before the word was coined."

The soldier-statesman would have been delighted to know that a descendant, Julia Gardiner, born on the island in 1820, married President of the United States John Tyler in 1844, becoming first lady of the White House at the age of 24.

Can You Say Mashashimuet?

Here's a pop quiz for all you Sag Harbor lovers. Where did the "Sag" in Sag Harbor come from? No, not from the shape of the bay or cove. And not from the shape of well-fed whaleship owners. Give up? A mainstay of the Indian diet on the South Fork was a tuber that grew underground in swampy areas. It helped feed the Pilgrims during their first precarious winter. Indians called the plant "sagga," which evolved into "sagg," before being adopted for Sag Harbor, a catchier name than "Great Meadows," which sounds like a condominium development.

Entrance to Mashashimuet Park, as it appeared on a postcard from the early years of the twentieth century.

Here's one you can spring on your friends in North Haven. Until 1842 that posh village was charmingly known as "Hog Neck" until several of its citizens decided to find something more attractive, sparing real estate agents from listing "a lovely five-bedroom in prestigious Hog Neck."

In 1992 a distinguished Sag Harbor historian, William Mulvihill, researched the derivation of names in and around the East End. He used many sources and credited particular inspiration from William Wallace Tooker who, until his death in 1917, studied the languages of Long Island Indians. Local place names are a reminder of our history and some of the people who were prominent in those early years.

Probably the first Indian name to pique our interest is one that everyone fumbles at first — Mashashimuet. In Algonquin it means "at the great spring" for the streams south of Otter Pond where heaps of shells and Indian graves have been found. The great Sag philanthropist Mrs. Russell Sage, on the advice of Mr. Tooker, suggested the word for the park she gave to the village.

Barcelona Neck, the 341-acre peninsula that runs from Rte 114 to Southwest Harbor and holds the Sag Harbor Golf Club, has an intriguing name but no one knows for sure where it came from. A sea captain claimed that the high terrain resembles that of the Spanish city, which seems a bit questionable.

Scuttlehole and Brick Kiln Roads link together and are colorful Early American names. Brick Kiln appears on maps as far back as 1690 when clay deposits along the road led to establishment of a brick-making business. Some of the clay pits became ponds. A scuttle hole was a trap door in the roof of a house that provided an emergency exit, especially when fireplaces were commonly used for cooking. But how do you get off the roof?

Accabonac is the Indian word for a place in Springs where those delicious tubers grew in abundance. It's a distance from Sag, but it gave birth to variations that we hear all the time. The short form, Bonac, refers to Springs and East Hampton in general and Bonackers are its proud citizens. Indeed, East Hampton High School sports teams are so nicknamed.

Many prominent citizens of Sag Harbor have been commemorated with street names. Of course they happened to be around when the community was expanding and new roads needed designations. Elegantly named Chatfield's Hill came from a family who supposedly were landed gentry in England. They never would have agreed to anything like "Hog Neck." There's a Cooper Lane in Southampton named for the Cooper clan that goes back to 1640. Its distinguished family members include Mercator, a whaling captain who reached Japan before Commodore Perry, and James Fenimore, the famous novelist and part-owner of the whaleship *Union*. His wife's cousin, Mrs. Charles T. Dering, lived in Sag and was related to the prominent Dering family that included Henry Packer Dering, Sag Harbor's first customs master and first postmaster.

The Corwin family lent its name to a road in North Haven and a street in Bridgehampton. Seth Corwin signed the 1842 document that changed the name from the aforementioned Hog Neck to North Haven. The Hunttings were a distinguished East End family descending from John, born in England in 1602, and lending their label to a lane in East Hampton and probably to the inn on its Main Street. Benjamin co-owned one of the early whaleships, and built the imposing mansion that became Mrs. Sage's summer residence which today is our whaling museum.

John Jermain was the grandfather of Mrs. Sage who put his name on the library she donated to the village in 1910. Her generosity gave Sag Harbor the tongue-twisting Mashashimuet Park, Pierson High School (named for her mother's family), and Otter Pond. She also established a foundation in Manhattan with $65-million she inherited in 1906 from her husband. Based on inflation tables, that's $1.5 billion in 2008 dollars, almost ho-hum today.

The large territory of Noyac took its name from an Indian word meaning "a long neck of land" which was obviously Jessup's Neck. In May 1777 Continental Army Colonel Jonathan Meigs sailed at night with 130 men in whaleboats from Connecticut to Noyac Bay. They crept down Brick Kiln Road, surprised the British in Sag Harbor, captured 100 prisoners, burned several ships and made a clean getaway. Jonathan didn't get a street name, but a modest plaque in the vicinity of Long Beach notes his exploit.

Countless parents have taken their little ones to feed blackcapped chickadees by hand at the Elizabeth Morton Wildlife Refuge at the base of Jessups Neck. The Wickatucks, a small branch of the Shinnecock tribe, farmed and fished there before the colonists arrived and are remembered by Wickatuck Drive off Noyac Road. No historical evidence has turned up that they closed the beach in summer to protect the piping plover.

Now that you're ready to impress summer visitors with your knowledge of local lore, think of leaning back after dinner and saying, "Interesting derivation for that name. Goes back to the Algonquins who…." Your guests will be dazzled and probably never come back.

Alexander Hamilton
Sued a Harbor Journalist

Since tickets to the hit show "Hamilton" are unavailable until around 2026, I won't know if the show mentions that David Frothingham, a former Sag Harbor newspaper editor, became enmeshed in the deadly feud between Alexander Hamilton and Aaron Burr. Living in Sag Harbor from May 1791 to December 1798, Frothingham was printer of the *Long-Island Herald*, Long Island's first newspaper. Mixed into this early American brawl and reflecting the bitter tone of politics at the time were the Alien and Sedition Acts passed in 1798.

Led by Treasury Secretary Hamilton and President John Adams, the Federalists pushed passage of the laws ostensibly to protect the country from foreign invaders, but opponents claimed the real purpose was to stifle a critical press that backed the Republican Party (also referred to as the Democratic-Republicans or the Anti-Federalists). Among the Republican leaders were Thomas Jefferson, James Madison, and Senator Aaron Burr who charged that the acts were unconstitutional, a threat to individual liberty and the First Amendment. Most historians absolve Hamilton from complicity in enacting the laws and portray him as a defender of civil liberties, but that didn't stop him from later suing Frothingham for libel and probably ruining his life.

In those days, newspapers boldly supported one side or the other. The *Long-Island Herald* owned by Henry Packer Dering and edited by Frothingham initially backed Hamilton's Federalists who favored closer relations with England. But Dering hated the British for plundering Long Island during the Revolutionary War and, in the summer of 1791, the *Long-Island Herald* printed Thomas Paine's *The Rights of Man* which took a sharp jab at England. Dering and Frothingham had begun favoring the Republicans and, possibly to avoid a fight with President Adams and Hamilton, Dering shut down the *Long-Island*

Annie Cooper Boyd house, which dates back to colonial times, now home of the Sag Harbor Historical Society.

Herald in 1798. Frothingham then went to work for the *New York Daily Argus*, the leading Republican journal, perhaps at the urging of Aaron Burr, Hamilton's long-time antagonist.

The First Amendment Center's Gordon T. Belt describes what ensued. In November 1799 the *Argus* reprinted an article that charged Hamilton with planning to purchase a Republican newspaper in Philadelphia in order to suppress its opposition. The critical article angered Hamilton who brought the matter to the attorney general of New York State, urging him to prosecute the owner of the *Argus* and its "foreman" David Frothingham for seditious libel. Frothingham was arrested and on Nov. 21st was charged with intention "to injure the name and reputation of General Hamilton, to expose him to public hatred and contempt, and to cause it to be believed that he was opposed to the Republican Government of the United States."

On December 3rd the court sentenced Frothingham to four months in prison, fined him $100 and stated he would remain in jail until the fine was paid and until he posted a $200 bond as a guarantee of good behavior. Prison was only the beginning of Frothingham's troubles. Writing in the August 1941 issue of the *Long Island Forum*, Nancy Boyd Willey, daughter of Annie Cooper Boyd, said, "There were rumors that he (Frothingham) was taken out west, and disposed of, along with other political prisoners."

Beatrice Diamond's 1964 book *An Episode in American Journalism* repeated this startling information, perhaps using Willey as a source. At any rate Frothingham was never seen again. After a period of thirteen years, his wife Nancy, believing her husband to be dead, married Daniel Latham. Mrs. Willey gave no source for such an astounding story and we have failed to uncover anything further. How are we to interpret "…disposed of, along with other political prisoners"? Did Hamilton have something to do with Frothingham's disappearance? Adding to the mystery, twenty-three years after his trial and disappearance, a Boston paper reported that a David Frothingham had died on the Congo River in Africa. Over 100 years later Louis Tooker Vail of Sag Harbor, intrigued by the story, asked Thomas Dewey, then district attorney for New York, for help in solving the mystery, but Dewey was unable to find any new information in State archives.

When Thomas Jefferson became president, he pardoned everyone convicted under the Alien and Sedition Laws, a correct decision for the country but too late to help Sag Harbor's former newspaper editor. After many years exchanging political and personal animosity, Burr killed Hamilton in a duel at Weehawken, New Jersey, on July 11, 1804, ending a tortured chapter in American history. We still don't know what actually happened to David Frothingham. Years later his daughter placed a memorial to him in Oakland cemetery which dates his death as 1814, but that is more guess than confirmed fact.

School Days in Colonial Times

There's so much controversy flying around about education and teaching that we found it fascinating to read an old issue of the *Long Island Forum* which carried an article describing colonial era schools. According to the writer, Nathaniel A. Howell, Southampton instituted the first school on Long Island in 1642, two years after English settlers came ashore at Conscience Point in North Sea. The first schoolmaster, Richard Mills, was also an innkeeper, "a fair penman and possessed a tolerable knowledge of arithmetic." No mention of a teaching certificate. Charles Barnes became the first schoolmaster in East Hampton, his salary of 30 pounds a year (about $150) paid in "beef, oil, pork, hides, tallow and whalebone."

Things were a little better for James Houldsworth who managed Huntington's first school in 1657. The town fathers agreed to build him a "sufficient" house and pay him 25 pounds in the form of "butter, merchantable trading wampum, well strung," or in commodities "as will suit him for clothing." Parents who sent their children to the school "should bring firewood…when ye seasons shall require it." At Setauket in 1687, Francis Williams's salary of 30 pounds was paid one-third by a tax on the people and the rest by parents of the scholars. One poorly paid teacher remarked, "It is little they pays and little I teaches them."

In her definitive history, *Sag Harbor: the Story of an American Beauty*, Dorothy Zaykowski wrote that the village built its first school house in 1786 on the corner of Madison and Jefferson Streets. She describes the space as "neatly papered" with wooden floors "scrubbed and sanded with beach sand every Saturday." In 1795 trustees Samuel L'Hommedieu, Henry Dering, and Noah Mason supervised schoolmaster Jesse Hedges.

According to Zaykowski's book, small private schools in Sag Harbor taught subjects not available in public schools, such as "navigation, surveying, advanced mathematics, and languages." In 1804 Major

John Jermain helped establish the private Middle School House at Church and Sage Streets. A Miss Leigh opened a School For Young Ladies in which girls "may be instructed in both the solid and ornamental branches of an English formal education." Solomon Parker started a school in 1807 for young gentlemen who "have a wish to render themselves qualified for the Navy of the United States or for the Merchant's Service...."

The *Long Island Forum* article noted that there were few books in colonial schools, and schoolmasters employed the Bible to teach the alphabet, spelling, and reading. Paper was a luxury, and when students could get it, they frequently sharpened their quill pens. Books were rare for over a century until the *New England Primer* was published in 1800, and Herman Daggett of Brookhaven came out with the *American Reader* in 1818. A Committee of Practical Teachers in Suffolk County published a common school arithmetic in 1850, announcing, "Arithmetic is founded on the fundamental principles of increase and decrease." An economist couldn't have said it better, or more succinctly.

Teachers thought that each printed page was so important that it should be memorized. "Spare the rod and spoil the child" describes discipline in those days. Hard to believe now but there were no dictionaries, so even teachers had difficulty in spelling. That's why early colonial documents contained wide variations in spelling and word usage, and illiteracy was so common that no one felt it was a disgrace. Some early practices bear an uncanny similarity to our modern world; wealthy families retained clergymen or other educated persons to tutor their young sons at home in preparation for college interviews, usually at Harvard or Yale.

Education of girls was considered unnecessary beyond the three Rs, but the Quakers thought otherwise, and in 1799 Harriet Beecher Stowe's Quaker mother ran a boarding school for young women in her East Hampton home. In 1813 NY State law created school districts with each town electing school commissioners and inspectors.

Cost per pupil in 1835 on the East End averaged $1.50; in 1872 it had increased to $7.00.

Desks in colonial schoolhouses took the form of rough, pine-board shelving built along the classroom wall with benches of long, backless boards. Sometimes wells were dug so that thirsty students could lift water in a bucket and dip a drink with a common ladle. One educator in the 19th century, Dr. Franklin Tuttle of Southold, made a fine point, "The true office of the teacher is not to instruct but to educate.... It is not his business to tumble facts into the child's mind as if it were a sunken lot to be filled up." Dr. Tuttle would seem to be on the side of today's teachers who argue against "teaching to the test."

Colonial Women Led a Hectic Life

You've heard the old rhyme, "Man may work from sun to sun, but women's work is never done." The writer, whoever it was, could have been describing housewives in Early America. On 18th century Long Island, meal preparation was a daily, time-consuming chore. Farm wives cooked in a chimney oven, or in the fireplace in iron pots hung from a trammel. Fireplace coals were banked at night to be stirred for the morning meal, otherwise one of the children went with a warming pan to a neighbor to ask for live embers. Milking the cows was a daily task, and cream from last night's milk was churned into butter. The mid-day meal featured salt meat, served first to the father and older sons so they could get back to the fields. On wash day, soft soap made from rancid fats and lye helped scrub clothes that were boiled for twenty minutes. On cleaning day, an attentive wife polished warming pans, candlesticks, and copper and brass kettles with a mix of salt and vinegar and a small amount of urine.

"Sam Porridge" was a favorite Sunday dinner, based on corn with beans, turnips, and if available, corned beef or salt pork. Colonials distilled birch beer from the bark of the birch tree. Candle making was a relatively pleasant chore involving saved up tallow scented with bayberry. These useful berries grew along the shore and the entire family enjoyed picking them for pies and cobblers. Apples were the favorite fruit, and pies made from dried apples might be the children's evening meal. They also were made into cider, applesauce, or apple butter. Some of today's vegetables weren't considered food but served other purposes — beets added color to dyes, lettuce soothed burns, string beans were an oddity, and tomatoes were considered poisonous. Potatoes only became popular after 1900. Long Island waters supplied an abundance of fish and shellfish, lobsters so plentiful and cheap that a housewife was embarrassed to serve them too often.

Most of this social history comes from *Around the Forks*, a collection of articles written many years ago by Edna Howell Yeager. In a section titled "Life In Earlier Times," Ms. Yeager describes childbirth in the 18th and early 19th centuries. In those days, she reports, when a father was informed that a birth was imminent, he took a skillet outside and whacked it with a spike. A neighboring woman, who knew the event was impending, answered with her own whacked skillet and relayed the news to other farms. The alerted women would grab their favorite nostrums and hasten to the side of the expectant mother where they would assist in the birth while discussing news of the community.

The attending women bantered possible names for the baby, Mehitabel most popular for girls, followed by Abigail, Keziah, Phoebe and Mary. The baby was fortunate if the mother's milk held out since many babies died for lack of food or from unpasteurized milk. Experienced mid-wives were in great demand. In the late 1700s, widow Lucretia Lester was said to have attended the birth of 1300 children, with the loss of only two. Birth was merely the beginning of danger and infant mortality was frequent. Cold houses, bad diet, poor medical help, and congenital weakness from frequent pregnancies often were fatal. The famous Cotton Mather and his wife Sarah had 15 children and only two survived him. The possibility of death led to immediate baptisms.

Sons were preferred offspring, to help on the farm, but daughters were welcome company for the mother as she taught them household skills. And there was a lot to learn. One critical skill was tending an herb garden, the Colonial source of health nostrums, beauty aids, and food seasoning. Folklore recommended skunk cabbage for asthma, honey and lobelia for whooping cough, wintergreen for rheumatism, and senna or dandelion for laxative. Spider webs stopped bleeding from a cut. Many herbs used then are still familiar today, sage for sausage, thyme for leg of mutton.

Spinning wheels spun all year long, small ones for flax, larger for wool. Once she accumulated enough yarn, the wife set up the loom to weave cloth, often "linsey-woolsey," an itchy combination of linen and wool. Woven, hand-dyed fabric went into clothing with every scrap saved for patches or quilts. Girls learned by stitching samplers.

Though modern women would say they still must fight to achieve equality, they'd surely agree they've come a long way since Colonial days.

✳ ✳ ✳

Christmas in Old Sag Harbor

A little hard to believe, but Christmas wasn't very popular in America until the mid-19th century. Early colonists, mostly Quakers, Baptists, and Puritans, viewed Christmas as an abomination, against their beliefs. But in the years after 1850, Christmas celebrations grew bigger, even getting a boost from President Lincoln who asked famous illustrator Thomas Nast to draw a picture of Santa Claus delivering gifts to Union soldiers. According to history blogger Tom Verenna, it was a not so subtle poke at the Confederates who were running out of the basic needs of daily life.

Ulysses S. Grant became president after the war and declared Christmas a federal holiday in 1870, hoping it would help solidify the newly reformed Union. You probably remember the response by editor Francis Church of the *New York Sun* to a letter from a young girl who asked if Santa Claus really existed. Published in 1897, it was headed "Yes, Virginia, there is a Santa Claus." It's still inspiring and it actually helped Christmas grow in popularity. Retailers caught on and enthusiastically joined in promoting the holiday (now well before Thanksgiving).

We now criticize the commercialization of Christmas, but in early years in Sag Harbor, December 25th was primarily a religious observance, and gifting and celebrating were usually modest and homespun. The December 28, 1893 edition of the *Sag Harbor Express* reported that at the M. E. Church on Christmas, Rev. James Coote called upon the Sunday school class for their gifts to the poor:

> ...now a long file of bashful young ladies... laden with potatoes and blushes, followed by young men bearing bags of flour, and bushels of vegetables, little tots with apples, oranges, and loaves of bread, older ones staggering under bundles of clothing and tons of coal, until the platform presented the appearance of a farmer's cellar, stocked for the winter.

According to *Child Life in Colonial Days* by Alice Earle, children's Christmas presents might have been a home-made hobby horse, a mask, a drum or a crude doll, and after much nagging by boys, a jack-knife. For outdoor enjoyment, according to the December 31, 1896 *Express*, "The ice having formed sufficiently thick to enable the boys to have their fun catching eels on Christmas Day...it looked like old times on Otter Pond.... We counted one day this week 35 persons 'at it' on the Upper Cove." Another winter pastime was ice skating brought to America from Holland by Plymouth pilgrims. The first skates on the frozen Hudson River were made of beef bones. Otter Pond saw scores of youngsters whipping over the ice, narrowly avoiding the eel fishermen.

The heyday of whaling peaked before Christmas became a major holiday, and according to ship logs we've seen, Christmas for whalers usually was a work day. The only exception might have been when the captain's wife was aboard, in which case the cook was urged to prepare something more than greasy pork, hard biscuits, and heavily salted beef or horsemeat. Life aboard a whaler must have been wearing on Mary Brewster on the whaleship *Tiger*. She wrote in her journal on Christmas 1848,

> I have passed a very pleasant Christmas tho' on board and nothing new around me, look where I will, the blue clouds and sea and faces so that they seem as familiar as old Ocean itself, 6 long months have I beheld them...surely I would not remain long could I help it but would be on land, by my own fireside and a prayer is often breathed, Oh God, preserve, prosper and return us to the land of our birth where may we live and die.

On the *John P. West* on Christmas 1882, according to the New Bedford Whaling Museum, Sallie Smith made popcorn balls. The lucky crew of the ship *Harvest* enjoyed seven turkeys and donuts fried in whale oil. One year the captain of a whaler sent a cheese to the crew (no insult intended). Another year, all hands received a mince pie. But most of the time there was no change in routine. Augusta Penniman aboard the *Minerva* in 1865 logged, "Genia [her son] hung up his stocking. Genia felt very anxious to know if they hauled back the main yard, and who took the boat's warp for Santa to get aboard."

One homesick sailor wrote a Christmas poem ending with the lines,

So weigh the anchor, set those sails
Don't slack along the way
With this good wind, unless luck fails
We'll be home for Christmas Day.

✳ ✴ ✳

Farming Was Big Business

in Colonial Sag Harbor

The proliferation of farmers' markets on the east end during the last few summers is a bit of a return to our colonial past. The South Fork was perfect for early colonists who came ashore at Conscience Point in Southampton from Connecticut and Massachusetts. Away from the beaches, the earth was a sandy loam ideal for growing bumper crops of wheat, corn, oats, hay, buckwheat, turnips, potatoes, cauliflower, and strawberries. Farmers easily gathered rich fertilizer from the beaches in the form of seaweed and menhaden, an oily, inedible school fish. Almost as important, farmers in 1675 raised horses, cattle, sheep, pigs, and chickens. America's first prairies were the 6,000 acres of grassy, rolling meadows of Montauk Downs, similar to the coast of Sussex, in England. We learned all this from Roger Wunderlich's article in the *Long Island Historical Journal* published in the fall of 2000.

To get away from hostile Dutch and British power centers in New Amsterdam and Boston, the colonists chose Long Island's east end and made a home in Southampton. This and other self-governing settlements established democracy, with issues decided by the people in a town meeting. Two hundred years later the state census of 1865 reported that farming was still the most common occupation but, reflecting the growth of towns and commerce, the census also recorded bakers, merchants, carpenters, shoemakers, teachers, and seamstresses.

The diary of Stephen Sherrill of East Hampton gives us a fascinating look at hard-working farm life in the mid-19th century. They plowed, planted, and threshed; harrowed, mowed, and husked; butchered hogs and steers; bought and sold horses, cows, and pigs; cut ice on the pond; carted guano, manure, and seaweed; clammed and fished; netted menhaden; repaired boats and mile-long nets, and went to church every Sunday.

The farmer had time for few distractions. On June 9, 1865, Sherrill wrote "went to the ice-cream shop with a couple of young ladies." On August 30th, he cut up corn while his brother "Nat and family went to…a watermelon party." On May 11th, "Damp day. Wind south and east. Whitewashed. Set two hens. Swore I would not whitewash again." But twenty days later, "Pleasant, whitewashed the kitchen and cultivating barn." As though he wasn't busy enough, Sherrill hired out as a workman. He cut ice for Abraham Dayton "for $2 per day, sold the old white cow to Jeremiah Dayton for $70. Put up wheat for the same Dayton at $2.35 per bushel. Sold a six-year-old Canadian mare for $150, and sold a load of hay for $80." He noted on December 2nd that pork had taken a fall in the market from 17 to 12 cents a pound.

Hamptons historian William Pelletreau wrote that by the 1870s the uninhabited Napeague stretch had become a village of fish factories, employing hundreds and selling trash fish far beyond the South Fork. Menhaden in the millions were rendered into oil and the remains used as fertilizer or, according to Wunderlich, shipped to enrich the vineyards of Italy (Do I detect subtle notes of menhaden?) and the cotton fields of the south. Many years ago when I worked as a summer "Parkie" cleaning the city beach in Rockaway, we called the fish "moss bunkers." When they washed up on shore we raked them into piles early in the morning and carted them away.

Innovations in agriculture paralleled the development of the railroad and telegraph. The reapers, threshers, and steel-bladed plows invented before the Civil War began to raise production. At the same time, the growth of urban markets led to a five-fold increase in harvesting of potatoes and the introduction of cauliflower, cabbage, and strawberries. During the 1880s and 1890s, competition from western wheat cut East End output in half. Besides vegetables and fruit, Sag Harbor also served as a port for two important cash crops sold in New York City — cordwood, the fuel of choice for heating houses before the coming of anthracite coal, and hay which fed the city's horse-drawn system of transportation.

In his book *The South Fork* Everett T. Rattray said that by the end of the 19th century artists and writers began coming out to enjoy the beauty of the Hamptons. The LIRR opened a line to Sag Harbor in 1869 and extended the track to East Hampton and Montauk in 1895. And so began the surge of summer visitors who now crowd the streets of the old whaling village and make ice cream cones our most lucrative product.

Bridgehampton Politics Were Wild

Are you still following politics and politicians? No, not Trump and Hillary and Sanders. I'm talking about John Adams and Thomas Jefferson and Alexander Hamilton. They were just as rough, and they fought with each other just like candidates do today. If you read about politicking as far back as 200 years ago, even in peaceful East End villages like Bridgehampton, you'll find that politics hasn't changed all that much. See if you can follow this tortured trail — In 1798, John Adams was president and tooling up to run for another term. Adams, a Federalist, planned to raise taxes to finance war with France because the French were attacking American merchant ships. The French were retaliating for the Jay Treaty which favored Great Britain. Opposition Republicans defied Adams's plan, citing the benefits of trade with the French and pointing at the harsh British occupation less than 20 years earlier. In fact the *Long-Island Herald*, published in Sag Harbor, asked in an editorial "Does there exist an independent American so lost to all recollection of the past conduct of the British government?"

The Federalist Party was America's first political party, formed by Secretary of the Treasury Alexander Hamilton while in George Washington's cabinet. The Federalists believed in strong central Government, a national banking system, and positive relations with England. Opposed to the Federalist Party were Republicans or Jeffersonians. Jefferson favored an agricultural economic base rather than one focused on banking, and was against closer ties with Great Britain. Since antagonists Hamilton and Jefferson were key members of Washington's cabinet, the partisan politics in the 1700s threatened to tear the new country apart. Sound familiar?

Jumping into the partisan fray were Bridgehampton Republicans who raised "Liberty Poles" to protest Adams's policies. Well-known Sag Harborite Henry Packer Dering owned the *Herald* and, though a staunch Republican, he worried about alienating Adams and perhaps losing his jobs as Collector of the Port and postmaster. So he closed down the paper. Ann H. Sandford, writing in the Fall 2002 *Long Island Historical Journal*, describes a Republican rally in December 1798 that drew supporters from all over Suffolk County:

> While warding off the chill from a northwest wind, the rally celebrants raised a seventy-six foot "Liberty Tree".... Mottoes, apparently carved into the trunk, read, "No unconstitutional act, no unequal taxes, Liberty of the Press, speech and sentiment...." The crowd sang the celebrated song of the Liberty Tree and its leaders raised their glasses and delivered patriotic toasts, perhaps enjoying rum bought at nearby Bull Head Tavern. They toasted the Tree of Liberty...the People of the United States...the Constitution .

Hundreds converged on the "Triangular Commons" in Bridgehampton, with the most cheers for Republican Vice President Thomas Jefferson (who became president in 1800). Apparently Bull Head rum overcame the northwest chill.

Aaron Burr, leader of the Republicans in the New York State Assembly and the next vice president, attended the rally and probably made a speech. On that day, the Triangular Commons served as a central meeting ground for jubilant Republicans just as it had for militiamen before 1776 and Independence Day celebrants after 1783.

The *LIHJ* article described the Triangular Commons as the center of Bridgehampton. In 1700, residents had worshipped at a meeting house located a mile or so south of the Commons, closer to the ocean and adjacent to the bridge that connected the Mecox and Sagaponack settlements and gave Bridgehampton its name.

A school, built farther north after 1720, and a new meeting house reflected the residents' confidence in the future of commerce as well as agriculture. Mercantile activity was becoming more valuable than ocean fishing and, because trade and communications largely used water routes through Long Island Sound and the Atlantic Ocean, merchants now depended on ports in the bays, including Sag Harbor.

By the 1790s, Bridgehampton boasted a church, school, library, tavern, post office, grist mill, and store, all within a half mile of its center. The federal government established the post office in October 1794 in — surprise surprise — the Bull Head Tavern on the northeast corner of the Triangular Commons. In 1800 the population likely numbered around 1,255, making it a substantial rural hamlet for its time.

By the way, the monument that today marks the center of the village was unveiled and dedicated on July 4, 1910 celebrating the 250th anniversary of the settlement of Bridgehampton.

3

Sag Harbor in War

Patriots Fled Sag Harbor
During the Revolution

Refugees? Displaced persons? You'd never think such terms would apply to citizens of Sag Harbor, but soon after the start of the Revolutionary War, the British won the Battle of Long Island fought in Brooklyn Heights in August 1776. They then occupied the entire island, and most American patriots on the East End fled to Connecticut and Westchester, losing their homes, farms, and possessions. As school children we had the impression that everyone in the American colonies was a Minuteman eager to fight the Redcoats. But historian Christopher Hamner says only a slight majority of the citizenry supported the Declaration of Independence and the break from the English crown. Fifteen to twenty percent of the population, called Loyalists or Tories, remained faithful to England, while the rest of the people sat on the fence and avoided declaring their allegiance.

Before the war, the infant town of Sag Harbor enjoyed growing importance as a commercial port. In 1772 a newspaper announced once-a-week stagecoach service from Brooklyn to Sag Harbor, along the way stopping in Hempstead, Smithtown, and Moriches. The route ended at Nathan Fordham's Inn on Main Street. "Thus," said the notice, "passengers may be conveyed 120 miles in three days on a pleasant road for 18 shillings" (about $2.25). But when war brought the British takeover, life became bleak. According to *Settlers of the East End* by Patricia Shillingburg, out of 32 dwellings in Sag Harbor, 14 men fled to Connecticut, roughly the same proportion seen in East Hampton, Southampton, and Shelter Island.

The recently built wharf at Sag Harbor saw many sad farewells. The effects of the occupation were disastrous. Refugees in Connecticut had no way to earn a living, while in Sag Harbor and neighboring towns the British army plundered crops and livestock even from Tories. One story, hopefully true, says that an abusive English officer, a Major

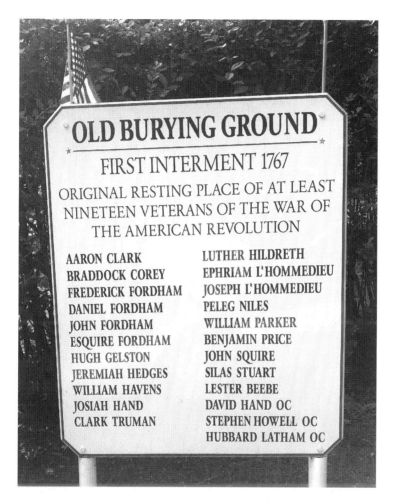

OLD BURYING GROUND

FIRST INTERMENT 1767

ORIGINAL RESTING PLACE OF AT LEAST NINETEEN VETERANS OF THE WAR OF THE AMERICAN REVOLUTION

AARON CLARK	LUTHER HILDRETH
BRADDOCK COREY	EPHRIAM L'HOMMEDIEU
FREDERICK FORDHAM	JOSEPH L'HOMMEDIEU
DANIEL FORDHAM	PELEG NILES
JOHN FORDHAM	WILLIAM PARKER
ESQUIRE FORDHAM	BENJAMIN PRICE
HUGH GELSTON	JOHN SQUIRE
JEREMIAH HEDGES	SILAS STUART
WILLIAM HAVENS	LESTER BEEBE
JOSIAH HAND	DAVID HAND OC
CLARK TRUMAN	STEPHEN HOWELL OC
	HUBBARD LATHAM OC

Revolutionary War veterans resting in the Old Burying Ground.

Cochrane, ordered whaling captain David Hand of Bridgehampton to turn out his team and cart to take a load of Cochrane's spoils to Southampton. Hand refused and Cochrane drew his sword. Hand grabbed a pitchfork saying, "I've fastened to many a whale and I'll fasten to you if you don't get out of here." "Well, Mr. Hand," said Cochrane, "I guess you and I had better be friends."

One motivation that drove men to the American cause was their cruel experience in the 1750s when they served in the ranks of the British army in the French and Indian wars. East Enders were not prepared for harsh treatment from British officers. At Ticonderoga, Long Island men had been ill-fed, ill-clothed and often beaten, a common disciplinary practice in the British army. They returned home full of fury at the English.

Sally Hedges remembered that her father kept a sow and pigs in his basement, and sheep and lambs in his bedroom to keep them out of the hands of British and outlaw marauders. Fences, buildings, and wood lots were taken for camp cooking fires, grains were stolen, and innocent people forced to give up family heirlooms and valuables. Homes, barns, warehouses, and wharves in Sag Harbor crumbled from lack of maintenance, while fields grew wild, tools rusted, and livestock were depleted.

At the end of the war in November 1783, formerly prosperous patriots, now penniless, returned from Connecticut with hatred for the Loyalists who had welcomed British rule. New American assemblies ordered Tories from their lands and homes. The Long Island Genealogy website says some 14,000 of them left New York for England, the West Indies, or Canada to avoid persecution. In 1783, 3,000 Tories from Long Island founded the city of St. John in New Brunswick, Canada. It took years to settle property claims and even longer for bitterness to fade on both sides.

One of the few bright spots for patriots was the raid led by Continental Army Colonel Jonathan Meigs. Deacon John White of Sag Harbor, a refugee in Connecticut, guided Meigs's force of 170 men (different sources report a somewhat different number) across the Sound from Connecticut. They portaged their whaleboats across the North Fork, crossed Noyac Bay at night, and surprised the British garrison in Sag Harbor. The raiders killed six Loyalists, destroyed twelve English vessels along with enemy supplies of hay, rum, and grain, and returned to Connecticut with 90 prisoners, all without the

Commemorating Col. Meigs raid in the Revolutionary War.

loss of a single man. The raid was a rare success during long years of suffering and loss on the East End.

Repelling Attacks in the War of 1812

In case you didn't notice, a few years ago we quietly celebrated the 200th anniversary of a Sag Harbor victory in the War of 1812. It wasn't a significant clash, not nearly as big as Andrew Jackson's triumph in New Orleans, but Sag Harbor militia did drive off a small British invasion force that landed at Long Wharf. 1812 was a strange war, with no clear reasons why it happened, or what was resolved, or who won. War hawks cited impressment of American seaman into the British Navy, and restraint of American trade with Europe as good enough reasons. According to a *New Yorker* article, "A British

97

government official compared the combatants to two men holding their heads in buckets of water, to see who would drown first."

Suffolk County saw little actual fighting but constantly feared attack because a British fleet under the command of Sir Thomas Hardy moored in Gardiner's Bay and made forays ashore to find fresh food and cattle. The fleet of eight warships also blocked commerce on Long Island Sound, halting profitable shipments of cordwood to New York City.

Sag Harbor was considered ripe for attack and General Rose of Bridgehampton requested ammunition for muskets, along with powder and a cannon. Local men formed into an artillery company with John Jermain as captain, and Elisha Prior, Cornelius Sleight, and Thomas Beebe as lieutenants. Captain Huntting commanded a company of infantry at the fort on Turkey Hill. Henry Dering was in charge of signals in case a landing should be attempted.

The *History of the Town of Southampton* by James Truslow Adams quotes a Mrs. Beaumont who witnessed the events.

> Many and many a time, both day and night, the alarm would be given "the British are coming." Then the wagons would be brought to take the women and children off in the oak timber, to stay until the cannon balls fired from the fort and wharf by our brave soldiers sent them back. I shall never forget that six weeks one summer all the women and children never undressed at night, but lay down with their clothes on, through fear of the foreign foe in the bay.

The British did indeed come, and General Rose's official report of July 11, 1813 dramatically described the encounter.

> Sir — About 2 o'clock this morning five barges from the British squadron came and made an attack upon Sag Harbor, took three vessels, set fire to one, but met with a reception so warm and spirited from our Militia there stationed, who

are entitled to much credit, as also many citizens of the place, that they abandoned their object and made a very precipitate retreat. They threw some shot almost to the extreme part of the place, but fortunately no lives were lost or injury done, except to the vessels which they had in possession, one of which was bored through and through by an 18-lb. shot from the fort. It is probable the enemy must have suffered, as they departed in such confusion as to leave some of their arms and accoutrements...."

Americans hatched ideas to use "torpedoes" on the blockading British ships, and Robert Fulton, later famous for his steamship designs, drew up plans which he presented to the U.S. Navy and to Congress. These were not the devastating torpedoes we remember from World War II, but more like mines that are still used today to scare off enemy vessels.

According to the New London County Historical Society, British captains were alarmed enough to frequently move their moorings to avoid being targets. Thomas Willing of Sag Harbor made plans, never realized, to tow out a mine and sink Captain Hardy's flagship *Ramillies*. Hardy huffily stated that the mines were "a mode of warfare practiced by individuals from mercenary motives, and more novel than honorable."

Besides Jackson's triumph in New Orleans which helped propel him to the presidency, the war is remembered for the torching of Washington, our hard-to-sing national anthem, the slogan "Don't give up the ship," and the duel between a British man-of-war and the American frigate *Constitution*. When a British cannonball bounced off its stout wooden hull, the *Constitution* earned the name "Old Ironsides."

What you probably never learned was that Nantucket suffered so from the British blockade that it made a separate peace with England, and five New England states actually considered secession, obviously not fully committed to federation. In view of such less illustrious incidents, it's better to remember the battle when Sag Harbor men stood fast and chased British invaders back to their ships.

✳ ✳ ✳

Terrible Bloodshed in the Civil War

The deadliest war in our nation's history began 150 years ago. The American Civil War killed over 600,000 men, more than the combined toll in all conflicts since then. War broke out in April 1862, when the Confederacy fired on Fort Sumter in Charleston Harbor, South Carolina. Historians cite different reasons for the hostilities, but the critical one was the practice of slavery that supported the plantation economy in the South.

Written in the florid prose of the time, the *Sag Harbor Express* printed a special edition on April 18th:

> WAR! The Civil War Has Begun! The agony of doubt and suspense has passed…. As we go to press the entire North is rushing to arms and the hearts of all are burning to avenge the insults heaped upon our flag.

On April 25th the *Express* published another special edition with a stack of headlines and exclamation points:

> THE WAR! Tremendous Excitement! Largest Meeting Ever Held in Sag Harbor! Every Man Ready! Recruiting Office Opened! 43 Volunteers Enrolled! Sag Harbor in the Front Ranks!

Reverend Edward Hopper of the Presbyterian Church was elected chairman of the town "meeting," and a committee solicited donations for "equipping our Volunteers and providing for their families while

The Civil War
monument
at Main and
Madison.

they are in service…. The Sag Harbor Cornet Band were present the entire evening and played many pieces which were thankfully received by the audience."

Reverend Hopper must have realized that everyone wasn't enamored of Abraham Lincoln. In a sermon on the following Sunday, he stated,

> We must forget party differences…the pilot at the helm may not be the one we helped to place there but when the ship is among the breakers we shall not stop to think of that…. When pirates attack the ship, we will not stop to ask whether the Captain is the man of our choice, but help him drive them back.

Local men served in a variety of military units, and many from Sag Harbor, Southampton and Bridgehampton volunteered for Company K of the 127th Infantry Regiment. The press reported that members of the regiment "pledged themselves to avoid as far as possible the prominent sources of immorality and discord usually connected with camp life and when they become soldiers not to forget their obligation as gentlemen."

Local novelist and historian William Mulvihill wrote that the 127th left for Staten Island in September, 1862, and later moved to Washington D.C. where they slept in tents through a wet, cold winter. Several men died from typhoid in February 1863, others from infections, dysentery, pneumonia, measles, and malaria. In April they bivouacked in Yorktown where they found clams, oysters, and crabs, a welcome change from hard tack and salt pork, and earning them the nickname, The Clamdiggers.

After marching all over the Mid-Atlantic States, seemingly at the whim of Union Army commanders, and having missed the war's most famous battles, the regiment sailed on August 7, 1864 to South Carolina between Hilton Head and St. Phillips Island. Its assignment was to blockade ports and cut the Savannah–Charleston Railroad that supplied Confederate troops blocking General Sherman's march to the sea. The 127th would suffer its greatest casualties in a number of little-known engagements.

That fall, John McMahon of Sag Harbor wrote to his wife, the former Elizabeth Slowey, that he had gone to confession and would receive communion the next morning. As part of a larger force, the 127th fought in the Battle of Honey Hill and was ordered to charge 30-foot high earthworks bristling with Confederate muskets and artillery. Two failed assaults ended in retreat to Bolan Church where surgeons worked through the night on the wounded and dying.

Official notices started arriving from the War Department, bringing sorrow to families in Sag Harbor and surrounding villages. Company K lost four men — Lyman Hedges, Harrison Norton, Joseph Corey, and John McMahon, who left Elizabeth and two children. He wouldn't live to see one of his grandsons become mayor of Sag Harbor many years later, in the 1950s. In another attempt to cut the railroad, at Devaux Neck, Charles Brown, Hy A. Skidmore, and Silas Halsey of Bridgehampton were killed. Dr. Charles Dayton of Sag Harbor, assistant regimental surgeon, was wounded but recovered and after the war cared for patients at his 1770 House in East Hampton.

Lists of the dead in the regiment continued to grow. Hiram Benjamin, 23, and Abram Loper, 19, killed at Coles Island. Jeremiah Payne, 22, died of wounds in a military hospital in Alexandria, Virginia. William Jacobs, 26, killed at Hilton Head. Stephen Squires, 21, killed at Morris Island. William Alberton, 33, killed at Folley Island. Jonathan Bennett, 20, died of wounds at camp hospital, Folley Island. William Harris killed at Hilton Head.

In February 1865 the Confederates retreated from Charleston and the 127th occupied the city. Lee surrendered to Grant at Appomattox on April 9th, ending the terrible carnage. Only days later another death shocked the country. Crazed actor John Wilkes Booth assassinated President Lincoln as he watched a play at the Ford Theater in Washington.

The 127th Infantry Regiment had left the North three years before with 1,000 soldiers, including men from Sag Harbor, Bridgehampton, Greenport, and Riverhead. Battlefield action, disease and harsh imprisonment killed 132 men. The regiment was mustered out, arrived by ship in New York City on July 7th, and marched up Broadway.

Later that month, Companies K and H took a train to Greenport for "a final celebration where young ladies sang, dignitaries gave speeches, and the veterans feasted in the shade of a pleasant grove." Home at last.

Our village monument on the south end of Main Street is modestly inscribed "In honor of the brave men who from Sag Harbor bore some loyal part in the Great Civil War." In May 1868, General John Logan proclaimed a day of remembrance to honor the dead on both sides of the terrible conflict. Initially called Decoration Day, it since became Memorial Day, a time to remember the men and women who sacrificed their lives in all our country's wars.

* * *

Harbor Boys Fought 100 Years Ago in the "War to End Wars"

You pass it as you drive up Main Street, the big rock topped by a bronze eagle on the edge of Otter Pond. A plaque commemorates hundreds of men from Sag Harbor who served in World War I, the conflict that began more than 100 years ago. A star next to a name means that the man died in service. There are nine of them. Many more suffered lasting wounds. An article in the *Sag Harbor Express* at that time asked the question "Will America Fight" and answered cockily, "Of course America will fight.... Once in the fight there can be but one result...victory for America."

But the brutality of war inevitably arrived home. Second Lieutenant Harold Braban Morris's 105th Regiment, 27th Division attacked the Hindenburg Line in September 1918 with terrible loss of life. He wrote:

> "In our own company there were barely 40 men left of the 250 man roster.... On October 17th we had only two officers and as the captain was wounded I had command of the company until gassed on the 18th. On the 19th the company was relieved having only eleven men and no officers.

Meanwhile the *Express* reported, the Junior Naval Reserve in "their new white uniforms" drilled on Sag Harbor's Main Street before several hundred spectators.

Corporal James Frederick Chelberg, born in Sag Harbor, served in the 306th Infantry of the 77th division. On September 6, 1918, his

The American Legion Post is named for Cpl. James Chelberg, killed in an artillery barrage in World War I.

company was on the front lines at the Vesle River near Reims, France when he was killed by German artillery. After the war, Chelberg's grieving mother searched military hospitals in the States, looking for someone who knew her son. She finally came across Charles Yerks who remembered James and told her about his last hours. The American Legion Post in Sag Harbor is named for Corporal Chelberg

The *Express* printed a letter from Stanley Heinricks "somewhere in France" to his mother and father in Sag Harbor.

> It is now five weeks since I have received any mail from you, but I suppose it's been tied up someplace…. the other night the Red Cross met our battalion…and distributed hot chocolate. It sure was good…. there were many dead Prussians

still lying around the fields and woods when we took over the lines...so we got busy and buried them...the Germans throw gas shells at us which in most cases consist of mustard gas... that takes effect on the skin...making blisters raise up and are very painful.

After the war, local boys were asked to report their experiences to Miss Emma L. Davis of Sag Harbor. One of them, Oscar Meyerson, served with the 307th Infantry of the 77th Liberty division. In the Argonne Forest his patrol captured six German soldiers and their machine guns. On March 8, 1918 William Jobe, still in the States, wrote, "Myself and 42 others have been transferred...to the Tank Corps and expect to leave for France any day.... You can tell the boys at home that they don't know what they are missing (if there are any left in Sag Harbor.)"

Seaman first class Wade French on the USS Cythera dodged German submarines in the Mediterranean. Corporal Rudolph DeCastro, an ambulance driver at a U.S. base hospital, wrote that the wounded were "more in danger riding in those ambulances than they were on the battlefield. We could not use lights...and would find ambulances off the road in a field or in a pond...." (In the Express, Sag Harbor's baseball team beat Orient and continued undefeated at 7 and 0.)

Both sides in the war used balloons for observation and Raymond John McIntosh attached to the 42nd Rainbow Division went aloft to spot enemy machine guns for American artillery. He was gassed in the Argonne Forest in October 1918 and wounded several times. But in his letter to Emma L. Davis he said "I still have two arms, two legs, and a damn good fighting temper." (In the Sag Harbor Express, leaders of the Women's Suffrage Movement are worried that the war will delay their cause.)

Seaman Joseph Theodore Biechele was a gun captain on the USS George Washington, a former German ocean liner, and made 17 voyages to Europe. On July 1, 1918 a U-boat attacked the convoy and sank the transport ship *USS Covington* with a loss of six men. At the end of the war, Biechele's ship carried President Wilson to the peace conference. (In the *Express*, ads promote Saxon cars for $395 and $795 "great for hill climbing, endurance, and speed.")

* * *

Local Women Served In World War II

Worrld War II involved everyone in America, including 70,000 women who volunteered in the Army and Navy Nurse Corps. A few of them in our community looked back at the war that ended more than 70 years ago. Hardly out of their teens, they stepped up to serve their country.

Frances Kalish as a young Army nurse had one of the more remarkable experiences of the war. She was born a Ruthinowski, grew up in Mattituck, and graduated from Southampton Hospital Nursing School in 1943. A year later, at age 21, she joined the U.S. Army Nurse Corps. She still remembers the crusty old sergeant who trained her and her sister nurses in Atlantic City. Immediately after boot camp, she sailed to England and France and was assigned to an army field hospital that was organized into three platoons, each with 60 enlisted men, six nurses, and six surgeons. To improve the survival of critically wounded soldiers, field hospitals brought major surgical capabilities closer to the front lines.

Frances's unit followed the Allied advance near Reims in northern France, caring for wounded GIs from fighting in the Ardennes Forest. One day, she was working from one stretcher to another, evaluating new arrivals and recording their condition. Suddenly, staring at the dog tags from a soldier who had been hit with shrapnel, she gasped in disbelief. "It was my brother, Stanley. I hadn't seen him in a couple of years and he had lost so much weight that I didn't recognize him.

We hugged and kissed despite his wounds. My commanding officer let me accompany Stanley for a few days to a hospital in the rear for further treatment. Thank God he recovered, but they needed men so badly that they sent him back into the lines."

Frances rejoined the field hospital as the Allies pushed into Belgium. Then late in 1944 the Germans broke through the American lines in a massive attack that became known as the Battle of the Bulge. "We didn't know what was happening. We took only essential medical equipment and retreated to a village near Bastogne where the 101st Airborne Division was holding out against heavy attacks. But we didn't panic, doctors and nurses and aides, we all worked together." The Bulge was the last desperate effort by the German army and in a month the Americans again were advancing.

Frances was discharged in the fall of 1946 and soon after married and raised four boys in Bridgehampton with her husband Connie. Of the war years, she says, "We simply did the best we could, a day at a time, and trusted in the Lord."

Dolores Zebrowski, a Sag Harbor girl all her life, always wanted to be a nurse and enrolled in the training program at Southampton Hospital in the early 1940s. She was born a Mulvihill, a well-known local family, and had attended St. Andrews Grade School and Pierson High. With her father a career Navy man and two brothers in the service, she volunteered for the U.S. Army Nurse Corps as soon as she graduated. After basic training in Fort Dix, the Army assigned her to Halloran Hospital on Staten Island where thousands of wounded soldiers arriving on hospital ships were evaluated for further treatment.

Hospital trains left from New York carrying the wounded to cities all over the United States. The trains traveled coast to coast, bringing the soldiers to communities and hospitals where they could best be cared for. Dolores made many trips all the way to the West Coast and, since she was junior in rank, often had the responsibility of night duty nurse for the entire train. "When the train stopped at some little town, local people would appear at trackside with food and coffee.

Sometimes one of the cars carried wounded German prisoners who were happy to be out of the war. Strange how some things stay in your mind — when we nurses requested it, the German soldiers would sing their sad, love ballad, "Lili Marlene" and we would all get teary."

In California, the medical staff brought wounded men aboard from the Pacific and began a reverse cross-country trip. She says proudly that in World War II over half the nurses in the United States volunteered for military service.

Anne Santacroce was operated on for appendicitis when she was a young girl living in Brooklyn. She must have received wonderful treatment because from then on she wanted to become a nurse. She couldn't have dreamed that ten years later she'd be caring for wounded American soldiers on the front lines in Europe. Born Anne Tedesco, she trained in nursing at Prospect Heights Hospital; further study at New York Hospital qualified her as an operating room nurse.

She was commissioned a lieutenant in the Army Nurse Corps in 1943 and was sent to Fort Dix where the Army formed hospital units before shipping them overseas. She sailed on the *Queen Mary* to Great Britain along with thousands of GIs, "everyone seasick the entire time."

After D-Day her hospital unit shipped out to France and later operated under tents outside Paris. As the allied armies advanced, her unit moved into Belgium to be closer to the front lines. "We worked 12-hour shifts, or longer when the fighting got heavy. Three surgeons operated side by side treating all kinds of awful injuries. The soldiers were young, 18 and 19 years old. I'll never forget one boy whose leg had to be amputated. I held his hand and cried with him. The wounded soldiers always asked us where we were from and when I said Brooklyn it was good for a laugh."

After the war, Anne returned home to work at the same Prospect Heights Hospital. Not much later she was introduced to Frank Santacroce from Sag Harbor whose sister had married Anne's brother.

She moved with Frank to Sag Harbor in 1949 and raised three children while working part-time at Southampton Hospital. Anne is proud of her service as an Army nurse but is sad that American boys are still being killed and wounded in far off lands.

Peggy Schwenk heard that the armed forces needed more recruits and decided to join the "Waves" in 1944 when she was 23 years old. Waves was the name given to women serving in the U.S. Navy. Born Margaret McCallen, Peggy left a job with General Electric in Schenectady and chose the Navy since her father had been a seaman in the First World War. At that time women weren't allowed in combat but they did important work that freed men for more hazardous duty. Women also were laboring in defense plants and factories, unheard of before the war. Peggy remembers that ration stamps were required to buy meat, eggs, and butter, as well as gasoline, but she says no one complained, everybody supported the war effort 100 percent.

At first, with her GE administrative experience, she was assigned a desk job at Navy Headquarters in Washington D.C. But she wanted to do more and volunteered for medical training at Hunter College in New York City, becoming a hospital apprentice first class. The Navy then sent her cross country to the Seattle Naval hospital where she tended wounded and sick men from the Pacific theater.

Peggy returned to civilian life in April 1946 and attended a community college in White Plains on the GI Bill, studying food preparation and nutrition. Twice a week she made lunch for other students, among them a young man from the Hamptons named Ralph Schwenk. Apparently he liked the food, and Peggy too. They romanced and married and raised a large family on the East End where Ralph had roots. They lived in North Haven for 43 years before moving to Bridgehampton. Ralph headed Rowe Industries in Sag Harbor and later ran a marina in Redwood. Peggy cherishes the letter of appreciation she received from President Harry Truman.

World War II from Brooklyn to Guadalcanal

B ill Connelie from Brooklyn volunteered as an aviation cadet in January 1942. The war wrenched him and hundreds of thousands of other young Americans from peaceful lives into dangerous adventures in places they never heard of.

After the sneak attack on Pearl Harbor on December 7, 1941, Japan's forces swept across the South Pacific and occupied Guadalcanal in the Solomon Islands. From an airfield under construction there, the Japanese planned to attack Australia and the New Hebrides. In August 1942, in America's first offensive action, U.S. Marines landed on Guadalcanal and began a long bloody battle to hold it against repeated assaults.

The Marines were still fighting Japanese hold-outs when Bill Connelie arrived on Guadalcanal in March 1943 with the U.S. Army Air force. Barely a year after he enlisted, the 21-year old was the navigator on a B-17 Flying Fortress operating from the island's patched up airfield. Bill and his crew hunted enemy submarines and bombed Japan's bases on Bougainville, Munda, and other strongholds. On most of his 60 missions, Bill's plane was attacked by Zeros, the famous Japanese fighter planes. He thanks the rugged B-17 for getting them safely back to base though full of holes from machine-gun fire. Every night the Japanese bombed the airfield to keep the Americans on edge.

In January 1944, the Air Force ordered Bill back to the States to train navigators on the new, long-range B-29 Superfortress. Practice flights from Puerto Rico to Norfolk, Virginia, roughly simulated the distance and direction the B-29s would fly from the Mariana Islands to Tokyo. During his military service, Bill rose from second lieutenant to major. After the war, he spent 30 years with the New York City Police Dept., reaching the rank of Assistant Chief of Department. He later became Superintendent of the New York State Police. Retired in 1983, Bill moved to Wickatuck Hills in Noyac.

Carmine Martino left his home in the Bronx at age 18, joining the Army Air Force in October 1943. He always had been fascinated by planes, built models as a youngster and hoped to become a fighter pilot. The Air Force sent him to Gulfboro, North Carolina, where he was devastated to discover his eyesight couldn't make the grade. Instead he was sent to Army schools to learn engine mechanics and airplane instrumentation.

He began working on B-24 bombers at Kessler field in Mississippi before being transferred to Selfridge Field, Michigan, where he serviced P47 Thunderbolts, powerful, new fighter-bombers built by Republic Aviation. Carmine helped train Free French pilots who came to Selfridge Field to check out the new planes, then flew them to Europe to fight the Luftwaffe. At one point in the war years, the famous African-American Tuskegee airmen took instrument training at Selfridge.

At war's end, after serving nearly three years, Carmine went back to his father's butcher shop in the Bronx while studying on the GI bill at NYU and CCNY for a teaching certificate. He concentrated on special education and later instructed teachers in that discipline in Brooklyn and the Bronx.

Andy Neidnig lived a quiet life before World War II, thinking only of finishing college and getting a job. A few years later he was fighting to survive, coming close to being killed battling the German army in Europe. Andy grew up in Ozone Park and graduated from Manhattan College in 1941. At that time, young men were required to serve a year in the military and Andy wanted to get it over with so he could move on with a career. He didn't know the Army would take five years of his life. Once the global war was underway, he was promoted to corporal and sergeant, then was sent to Officer's Candidate School at Fort Benning, Georgia. Eager for action he was shipped to an infantry unit in the Second Armored Division that was advancing into

Germany in 1944. He no sooner joined the division than the Battle of the Bulge erupted and his unit raced into position to block the German advance.

They confronted elite Panzer divisions in Belgium in bloody fights with the outcome in doubt for over a month. On Christmas morning, 1944 Andy had hitched a ride on a Sherman tank when a shell hit the tank and sent him flying. A little later while talking to another officer he heard a sniper bullet zip by his head. They captured the sniper and found he was wearing American Army boots, probably from a fallen soldier. His closest brush with death was near a small Belgian village. He was walking alongside a Sherman tank when it was hit by a rocket from a "panzerschrek", the German version of our bazooka. A huge red flash knocked out the Sherman tank and killed his captain.

Out of his company of 60 men, 48 were killed or wounded. In the fiercest winter of the war, men who fell froze in position. Andy jokes that while he was sleeping on icy ground, Army regulations took $30 room and board from his lieutenant's salary of $175 a month. The Bulge broke German resistance and the European war ended a few months later. He and his buddies were apprehensive, expecting orders to the Pacific for the invasion of Japan, but the A-bomb ended the war.

Andy remembers his homecoming as a quiet reunion with his family, without fanfare. He says he thinks frequently about his experiences so many years ago when his only hope was to survive. He and his wife moved permanently to their home on Glover Street in 1982.

Marty Trunzo, whose real first name is Mario, was born in Calabria, Italy, and arrived in the U.S. at age 11. He didn't realize he'd get a free trip back not many years later, courtesy of the U.S. Army. Marty's Barber Shop opened on Main Street in 1930 where he groomed Sag Harbor men until he was drafted in April, 1942. After boot camp at Fort Dix, Marty joined the 389th Port Battalion attached to the 36th Infantry Division.

"I asked an officer why they had us climbing up and down rope nets. He said just to keep you in shape. Next thing I knew we were invading North Africa. That wasn't so bad. It really got ugly when we landed at Anzio in Italy. The Germans had a huge railroad gun we called the Anzio Express, and they pinned us down for months, inflicting terrible casualties. When I got ashore an Italian Army captain said 'Where have you been? We've been waiting for you.'"

As the war neared its end, Marty, then a sergeant, was put in charge of the Hotel Picha Cusa on Ischia, an island near Capri that the Americans had taken over as a rehab center. When he was told that an American general was arriving for inspection, Marty commandeered a weapons carrier and sped to a fishing village where he exchanged GI rations for fresh seafood. After a delicious dinner, the general asked Marty how he was able to turn out such a splendid meal. Marty confessed his bartering excursion. The general said, "Well okay, just don't get caught."

Marty's worst experience came after the shooting stopped. A little Italian boy playing in the rubble picked up a German mini-bomb. It exploded and he was bleeding profusely. Marty rushed him to a hospital where they were able to save his life, but the boy lost his hand. Marty shakes his head in sadness when he tells the story.

World War II Saboteurs
Landed at Amagansett

In 1942 a U-boat landed German saboteurs on the beach in Amagansett. Their mission was to blow up aluminum plants and key transportation hubs. Another group of saboteurs came ashore on Ponta Vedra Beach in Florida. Only six months at war, America had suffered disastrous defeats in the Atlantic and Pacific theaters. Fortunately, the vaunted German war machine committed serious blunders in the sabotage attempt. Punishment for the invaders harked back to legal decisions by Abraham Lincoln, involved the U.S. Supreme Court and presaged George Bush's "war on terrorism."

Michael Dobbs, a reporter for the *Washington Post*, tells the story in *Saboteurs: The Nazi Raid on America*. Concerned about America's industrial might, Hitler ordered the strike only a couple of months before. In a hurry to obey the Fuhrer, Walter Kappe, a former official of the German–American Bund, selected men who had lived in America, only two of whom were German soldiers.

The Bund was an American-Nazi organization of German immigrants that flourished in the 1930s. Kappe split the recruits into two groups of four each and gave them a meager five weeks of training. John Dasch headed one team while Eddie Kerling led the Florida contingent. It made sense to find men who were familiar with the States, but a proper vetting would have revealed that most of them were reluctant warriors, and a couple, including Dasch who had worked as a waiter in the Hamptons, had no intention of carrying out sabotage.

The two groups carried false identification papers and large amounts of cash. The Florida landing went easily and the team buried munitions for later retrieval. Amagansett was another story. On a foggy, moonless night, using his quiet electric motors, U-boat Captain Linder crept up to the beach until the sub touched sand, then sent the saboteurs ashore in a rubber dinghy. In an uncanny bit of luck, along came U.S. Coast Guardsman John Cullen who had worked at Macy's until Pearl Harbor. "Who are you?" yelled Cullen. "Fishermen from East Hampton," yelled back Dasch. Cullen was suspicious and asked them to accompany him to the Coast Guard Station. Dasch refused, threatened Cullen and stuffed a wad of money in his hand. Cullen took the cash and ran back to the station.

Boatsman's Mate Carl Jennett and his crew followed Cullen back to the landing spot, but saw only the submarine stuck on a sandbar. Jennett called Coast Guard headquarters in New York City and two lieutenants began driving to Amagansett. No one took Cullen's story seriously. Meanwhile the Germans walked to the Amagansett Railroad Station and caught the 6:59 am to Penn Station, changing at Jamaica like dutiful commuters. Once in the city, they checked into hotels and shopped for clothes at upscale Rogers Peet Department store.

Dasch and Burger contacted the FBI's New York office but the man on duty filed the call as crazy. Dasch then headed for Washington D.C. He called Hoover but was switched to agent Duane Traynor who had heard about Amagansett. With Dasch's information, the FBI quickly picked up the three other members of Dasch's squad, and by the end of June arrested the Florida men as well. Characteristically, Hoover grabbed all the credit, announcing the arrests without consulting other Government departments and without mentioning Dasch's vital role. President Roosevelt was adamant about the fate of the saboteurs, "I won't hand them over to any U.S. Marshall armed with a writ of habeus corpus."

FDR agreed to a military commission rather than a court martial which would offer the Germans more protection. Army Colonel Kenneth Royale, assigned to defend the Germans, turned out to be a courageous advocate and asked FDR for a civilian trial. Instead the commission held procedings in secret, making up the rules as they went along and defeating any motions by Royale. The Justice Department ordered the dismissal of German, Italian, and Japanese waiters in Washington D.C. lest they overhear any secrets from diners.

Royale appealed to the Supreme Court, citing a court decision in 1864 that Lincoln's suspension of habeus corpus in the Civil War was unconstitutional. "Habeus corpus is one of the most venerable legal procedures in the Anglo-Saxon world," wrote author Dobbs. "It prevents authorities from holding people unlawfully by demanding they be turned over to a legally constituted court." None of the Supreme Court justices was willing to dispute the war powers claimed by FDR, though Frankfurter noted, "The justices had agreed on a verdict without agreeing on the reasons for the verdict, a reversal of normal procedure." William Rehnquist later said both Lincoln and FDR valued prosecuting war more than obeying the constitution.

The commission sent FDR a decision of death by electrocution, but recommended clemency for Dasch and Burger. Four executioners received $50 for each execution. The remains of the six saboteurs were taken to a graveyard for unclaimed bodies and marked only by numbers on headboards. A number of Bund members and families who had been in contact with the spies were tried and sent to prison, but released in the 1950s.

Harry Truman pardoned Dasch and Burger in 1948 and they were deported to Germany. Burger was employed by Bayer Pharmaceuticals and sent Chistmas cards to Hoover. Dasch wanted to get back into the U.S. but was thwarted by Hoover. He died in Germany in 1992. Eventually Walter Kappe, who recruited and trained the saboteurs, ran a souvenir shop outside the American Army base in Frankfurt.

After 9/11 President Bush suspended habeus corpus for "unlawful enemy combatants" citing Lincoln's and Roosevelt's actions.

World War II Washed Ashore
on Long Island Beaches

During World War II, I lived near the ocean on the south shore of Long Island, close to New York Harbor. The beach was my playground and I often browsed the shoreline to see what the waves had washed onto the sand. Within weeks of the attack on Pearl Harbor, after Germany joined Japan in the war against the U.S., something new showed up along the high water mark. Mixed with the familiar driftwood and clumps of seaweed were life jackets, hundreds of olive-colored cans, and globs of congealed oil that stuck to my feet. Markings on the cans identified them as C-rations, the loved and hated provisions intended for American soldiers overseas. Most of the cans I found contained chocolate bars, powdered coffee, chewing gum and little cigarette packs which led some of my buddies to take their first hesitant puffs. It dawned on us that the C-rations probably came from allied ships torpedoed just off the Atlantic shore.

In his book *Mayday*, author Van Field says that when war broke out, German Admiral Karl Donitz ordered submarines, referred to as U-boats, to interrupt shipments of war materials from the U.S. to England and Russia. Fortunately Hitler had other priorities for the submarine force and Donitz could spare only five of the craft to range along our East Coast. I say fortunately because that handful of German subs sank 25 ships in January 1942, most of them within sight of land. Thinking America was too far away to be affected, merchant ships and tankers in those early months of war sailed with their running lights on, silhouetted against a brightly lit coast, making them easy targets for U-boat kapitans.

Most of the sinkings were in busy sea lanes off Nova Scotia, Cape Hatteras, and Florida, but on January 15, 1942, U-boat 123 sank the 6,700-ton tanker *Combria* off Long Island, her cargo of oil illuminating the sky near Shinnecock Inlet, her 36-man crew drowned or burned to death. The day before, the same submarine torpedoed

The World War II monument in Marine Park.

the 9,577-ton tanker *Norness*, 60 miles southeast of Montauk. The German captain had only a tourist map of the New York area, but was able to take navigational fixes from the still-operating Montauk Point lighthouse.

The January 14th *New York Times* blazoned the *Norness* story across the front page and carried the sub-head, "Navy Says Peril Extends Pretty Well Up and Down East Coast." U-boat 123 was a long range, diesel-driven craft able to travel at 18 knots on the surface, and, propelled by batteries, a little over seven knots submerged. Prime targets were tankers sailing up from Caribbean and Gulf Coast oil ports. According to author David Kennedy's *American People in World War II* a single U-boat off New York Harbor sank eight ships, including three tankers, in just 12 hours.

For months we found debris from sinkings all along the shore. The U.S. responded feebly with old, wooden subchasers, antique aircraft and a flock of private yachts dubbed Hooligan's Navy. The carnage continued until Admiral Ernest King, the top U.S. Naval commander who hated everything British, reluctantly took their advice and introduced a convoy system, greatly reducing losses and even sinking a few of the German attackers. In August that year Donitz reassigned the subs to other parts of the Atlantic. The tally — in 1942, 121 ships were sunk off the East Coast; in 1943 the number dropped to 22.

Casualty reports of the submarine war vary depending on sources, but a best estimate is that in the Atlantic alone, from late 1939 to 1945, U-boats sank over 2400 cargo ships and oil tankers, representing 18-million tons of shipping. Civilian crews that manned the ships are seldom mentioned as war casualties, but in fact, according to the American Merchant Marine Association, over 9000 merchant mariners lost their lives, a higher casualty rate than regular military forces. When peace came, Winston Churchill admitted that the submarine threat frightened him more than anything else during the global conflict. If the Germans had built more submarines earlier, they might have completely cut off supplies of war materials to England, Europe and Russia, and Hitler could have won the war.

As innocent kids, picking through the remains of sunken ships along the Long Island shore, we were only vaguely aware of the terrible sacrifices men and women were making to preserve our freedom.

Harbor Vets Talk about Vietnam

The three friends had all graduated from Pierson High School, then fifty years ago served in the war in Vietnam that killed 58,000 Americans. On Veterans Day, regardless of our opinion of the war, regardless of our political leanings, we honor them and the scores of other Sag Harbor men who answered their country's call. We asked a few of them to describe their experiences.

Paul Babcock graduated from Pierson a couple of years ahead of Bob Ratcliffe and Bruce Winchell. The three young men knew each other in Sag Harbor. Vietnam created a bond and a respect among them, and each man said the other two saw tougher combat.

"I graduated from high school, earned a degree from Lafayette College, then joined the Air Force, just days ahead of a draft notice. I went through OCS, took flight training at Laredo Air Base, and also at the forward air control special ops school at Hurlbert Field, Florida. That's where I learned to fly the Cessna 01E. Nicknamed the Bird Dog, the little, single engine 01E had none of the glamour of supersonic jets, but its mission had its own challenges.

"I arrived in Vietnam in October 1968. My first assignment was north of Bien Hoa Air Force Base at a small strip called Song Be. I often flew at night when the Viet Cong were most active, and saw tracer fire rising towards my plane. The enemy hated the Bird Dog and 469 of them were lost in Nam. I remember meeting Bruce Winchell at Bien Hoa over a bottle of Drambuie, the night a rocket attack blew up the munitions dump. Another night, the VC overran Song Be, throwing satchel charges which killed the base commander and his staff. I held out in a bunker with a number of enlisted men and medical personnel. We barricaded firing ports to keep out the satchel explosives.

"After six months at Song Be, I was assigned to General Abrams' Third Mobile Strike Force. One day, supporting a battalion in a hot fight with the enemy, I flew for hours under a thick fog at about 300 feet, calling in artillery and gunships. War can be horrific. In retrospect, the conservative values and the ethics of freedom I learned and which surrounded me as a youngster in Sag Harbor, helped me get through my tour of duty and through the toughest battles. When my year in Vietnam was up, I returned home and for a while instructed on the C141 multi-engine cargo plane. I left the service in spring of '73 and flew for Eastern Airlines."

(On the recommendation of the battalion commander, Paul was awarded the Silver Star for gallantry in action.)

Bob Ratcliffe, the youngest of the three veterans, joined the Marine Corps on a youthful whim. He was the only one to volunteer for a second tour and his reasons give us a small sense of the violent stresses of combat.

"I graduated from Pierson in 1965, attended Snow College, and went to work for New York Telephone Company. With the draft on, I tried to enlist but was rejected because I still had effects of childhood polio. One day a Marine recruiter in dress blues came into a diner in Riverhead where I was having lunch and I decided right there to join the Marines. Hell, I was still a kid. They offered something called an Air Wing Guarantee and sent me to school in Memphis to study jet mechanics. Instead I switched orders with a buddy who had a wife and child and I became a crewman on the Boeing CH46 twin-rotor helicopter. After further training at Camp Pendleton I went to Nam in 1968.

"My unit, HMM 263, which means Helicopter Marine Medium, was stationed in Marble Mountain, an air facility outside Danang in the I Corps area. It extended from the DMZ in the north to Chu Lai in the south. I manned a 50-caliber machine gun on a chopper that performed medevac and resupply for the 26th Marine Regiment. The hairiest times were getting recon teams into hot landing zones, or pulling them out, especially at night. We always were attacked from the surrounding tree line and I'd lay down suppressing fire with the fifty. I can still hear AK-47 rounds ripping through the skin of the chopper.

"My first tour was 13 months, but I volunteered for another year. I was uncomfortable at home, missed my Marine buddies and, to be honest, I missed the rush you get in battle. Sounds crazy but like other guys I probably had what everyone now calls PTSD. It leaves a mark. I finally mustered out of the Marines in 1971 and went back to NY Tel. When I retired I became caddie master for a few years at Atlantic Golf Club. I now run an estate management company."

(The Marine Corps awarded Bob a single-mission Air Medal with Bronze Star for action outside Hoi An.)

Bruce Winchell was the only one of the three Sag Harbor boys to see combat on the ground as an infantry "grunt." In a moment of reflection, he defined courage in battle as a constant struggle between the instinct for self-preservation and the resolve to do your duty. Indeed all three of the Sag Harbor men did more than their duty and were decorated by the military for their courage under fire.

"I landed in Vietnam in late 1967, just before North Vietnamese Army regulars launched the big Tet offensive. My unit of the 101st Airborne Division had recently arrived near Hue in the north, and we got pitched into one of the war's bloodiest battles.

"My father had served in the military and I enlisted at age 19, just out of Pierson High School, class of '65. I was lucky to take advanced infantry training, and paratrooper and Ranger training before I went to Nam. I made staff sergeant and became a squad leader in a recon unit whose job was to locate the enemy. My biggest worry was to make sure my squad had enough ammunition, water, and food. Tet actually was a military victory for American forces, but heavy casualties shocked people at home and turned them against the war.

"After Tet, we pushed the enemy towards the Laotian border. The bitter combat in the first three months of '68 still haunts me. NVA regulars would pop out of 'spider holes' at any second, firing AK-47s at close-range. A mortar shell killed my assistant squad leader, a kid from Torrance, California. At one stage we wore ponchos. Not for rain. They could be used as body bags if we were killed or wounded. Patrolling in the A Shau Valley, we came under heavy fire and I was shot in the knee. After treatment in Japan, I went back on the line. In August I was wounded in the other knee during a mortar attack. Once patched up, I was assigned to Bien Hoa Air Force base outside Saigon where I trained newly arrived soldiers, trying to teach them to survive.

"Bien Hoa was supposed to be quiet, but wasn't. A Sag Harbor pal, Paul Babcock, and I were having a drink late one night when a rocket attack hit the base munitions dump and lit up the sky. I returned home before Christmas 1968, and was surprised by anti-war demonstrators in San Francisco. They blamed the soldiers when they should have blamed the politicians. I now run a marine engine business in Noyac."

(The Army awarded Bruce two Bronze Stars to go with his two Purple Hearts.)

4

Living With the Sea

Did a Lighthouse Wreck the *John Milton?*

Professional seaman are familiar with NOAA's publication, *Notice to Mariners.* It warns of new hazards or changes to navigation aids which didn't appear on the latest charts. If only the National Oceanic and Atmospheric Administration had existed in 1858. If only it had issued a notice about the new Shinnecock lighthouse. If only the captain of the sailing vessel *John Milton* had received the notice, then the crew and passengers of the 1445-ton ship wouldn't have died in freezing waters off the south shore in one of Long Island's worst maritime disasters. If only.

When you drive south through Hampton Bays towards the Ponquogue Bridge and the barrier beach, you pass the U.S. Coast Guard Shinnecock Station on the left just before the bridge. On this site in 1857, before the Coast Guard base existed, the Government erected a lighthouse. The tower was 160 feet high, built of red brick. Fueled by lard oil, the light shone through fine glass lenses imported from France and could be seen 20 miles at sea. The first keeper, John Hallock, and his two assistants lived in houses at the base of the tower. Coal for a stove and oil for the light were hoisted up outside the tower by heavy rope. The light began operating on January 1, 1858, a boon to the safety of mariners. Or so everyone thought.

After a voyage of nearly three years, touching at San Francisco, Peru, and finally Hampton Roads, Virginia, the three-masted, 203-foot *John Milton* departed for her home port of New Bedford, Massachusetts, on February 16, 1858. Strong northeast gales and heavy snowstorms battered the ship as she clawed past Cape May. The mercury dropped to eight degrees above zero. Sometime during the night of the 19th, Captain Ephraim Harding no doubt was relieved to see a steady beam over his port bow. Ah, he thought, Montauk Point. What the captain couldn't know was that the bright beam came from the new Shinnecock lighthouse, and Montauk's light was still far off. In the blinding storm, forging ahead and thinking he was well clear of the island's end, he turned to a more northerly course for New Bedford. But the *John Milton* never reached its home port. At 10 am on the 20th, the ship piled up on the rocky Montauk coast in the section known as Ditch Plains.

Near evening, bodies floated ashore frozen and covered in ice. The *Sag Harbor Corrector* (predecessor of the *Sag Harbor Express*) of March 11, 1858, reported,

> The first that was discovered was a boat bottom up, and near it, was a body, on the shore, and a little to the eastward, the wreck was discovered. The bows, bowsprit, head gear, etc. was discovered about one third of a mile from shore, probably held there by her anchors; the rest of the wreck was scattered along the beach; heavy masts and spars came ashore, broken and twisted up in several pieces....

By marks made in the sand, witnesses deduced that the ship's cook had made it to the beach and attempted to crawl from the water, but froze to death before help arrived. The coroner held an inquest in a barn on Newtown Lane in East Hampton.

Local authorities brought recovered bodies over snow-bound roads to East Hampton where on February 28th they arranged a funeral service in the old Presbyterian Church across from Clinton Academy. Montauk historian Henry Osmers wrote a book about the disaster, *They Were All Strangers: The Wreck of the John Milton at Montauk, New York*. The title came from the words of Captain Thomas Mulford who spoke at the service. Twenty-one victims rest in East Hampton's South End Burying Ground where a monument remembers their fate. Captain Harding and his teenage son were buried in Tisbury, Mass., and other victims were taken to graves near their family homes. Different sources put the number of dead at 32 or 33. The ship's bell was retrieved and tolled for years from the Presbyterian Chapel known as Session House. It is now part of the collection of the Montauk Lighthouse Museum.

In 1934 the Government erected an electric beacon on a metal framework on the ocean beach in Shinnecock and the lighthouse no longer was needed. It was offered to Suffolk County for one dollar but the County turned it down and it was demolished in December 1948.

An article in the April 1944 issue of the *Long Island Forum* described the tragic role played by the lighthouse in the wreck of the *John Milton*.

※ ✳ ❊

Even Computers Can't Predict East End Weather

According to Mark Twain, "Everyone talks about the weather but no one does anything about it." In fact, a *New York Times Magazine* article about weather quoted a specialist who headed the National Hurricane Center during Katrina. He said, "Uncertainty is the fundamental component of weather prediction." One supercomputer used for atmospheric research can make 77 trillion calculations each second, yet a National Weather Service director admitted "there are still things that computers can't do." Though we're tempted to say "Duh!" to both statements, the complex science of weather prediction actually has gotten a lot better.

Weather variations on the East End give us plenty to talk about, below freezing in winter and stifling hot in summer. In a quick rundown of the worst storms to hit Long Island, you always start with the Great New England Hurricane of September 21, 1938, which blew the steeple off the Old Whalers Church. No one prepared for it because a Category 3 storm hadn't come ashore in over 100 years. According to the *Farmer's Almanac*, gusts reached 186 mph and the ocean surge was 17 feet. I watched in awe from an ocean-front apartment in Rockaway

Beach as waves broke over the boardwalk and rushed down the street into Jamaica Bay.

Not many years later, the Great Atlantic Hurricane (they didn't start naming them until 1953) came ashore between Southampton and Westhampton and knocked out power for ten days. Hurricanes Donna in 1960 and Gloria in 1985 were Category 2 storms, meaning sustained winds of 96 to 110 mph. Bob crossed Montauk on August 19, 1991, with winds of 101 mph, ripping up bulkheads along Little Peconic Bay in Noyac.

According to an earlier *New York Times* article, experts claim the Saffir–Simpson scale that ranks storms in "categories" can be misleading to shore-side residents because it is based on the power of the wind, and doesn't include ocean surge. In response, NOAA says that surge varies widely depending on coastal conditions, and recommends explicit warnings from the National Weather Service to support decision-making at local levels. Helping with regional data was Bridgehampton's centenarian Richard Hendrickson, a local weather observer for the NWS for 80 years. (Hendrickson died in 2016 at the age of 103.)

Hurricane season officially runs from June 1st to November 30th and peaks in early September. Hurricanes aren't the only worry for Eastern Long Island. Every few years an intense storm, usually a nor'easter, brings nearly as much wind, rain, and tide. The "Halloween Storm" of October 31, 1991, hit Long Island with 60 mph winds and waves so high they were detected by Cornell's seismograph in Ithaca, New York. We owe that fact to Norm Dvoskin writing in a 1992 issue of the *Long Island Historical Journal*.

The first two weeks of February bring the most snow, according to the American Meteorological Society (AMS). The largest storm in New York City history dumped 26.9 inches of snow on February 11, 2006. The East End's proximity to the ocean usually tempers snowstorm effects, changing precipitation to rain and sleet. But that wasn't rain we shoveled during the hard winter of 2010–2011. Dvoskin reported historic snowstorms including one in 1857 when the *Sag Harbor Corrector*, forerunner of the *Express*, didn't get its shipment of newsprint and had to put out an issue on brown paper.

The "Blizzard of 88" is the benchmark for winter storms, bringing powerful winds, bitter cold and 33 inches of snow to Patchogue. That would trump the 2006 storm, but apparently the weather gurus consider 1888 ancient history. More recently, the snowiest single month was February 2010 with a 36.9-inch accumulation, and the 95–96 season which piled up 75.6 inches.

In general the North Shore gets the most snow on Long Island, mainly between Port Washington and Port Jefferson. The least amount falls along the South Shore, especially the barrier islands. Many variables account for the differences. The ocean has a modifying effect, except for nor'easters. The East End only gets more snow when the storm track is well offshore. New York City's "heat island" reduces snow on that end. A small "lake effect" from Long Island Sound and an abrupt change in elevation, though modest, contribute to the snowier North Shore.

They Hanged Captain Kidd

Captain Kidd's name is as familiar today as it was 300 years ago. Part of his continuing fame is the mystery of his treasure, at least some of it buried on Gardiner's Island off East Hampton, or the notoriety of his trial before the English House of Commons, or the fact that he was hanged for crimes he may not have committed. In his well-researched book, *The Pirate Hunter*, Richard Zacks details all of these possibilities. Like any good historian, he tells it like it happened, yet between the lines you detect the author's feeling that Captain Kidd got royally shafted.

William Kidd was born in Dundee, Scotland, January 1654. By the late 1600s he had become a respected citizen of New York City, then a struggling seaport of 5,000 people, with a handful of paved streets and the one sanitation man assisted by hungry pigs. Kidd was captain of a merchant ship and happily married to Sarah, a young, wealthy widow. He could have led a comfortable life, but he was adventurous and naively decided he should become a captain in the British Royal Navy.

With a recommendation from a friend, he sailed to London, but got a cold shoulder from the Admiralty. Instead he fell in with politically connected Robert Livingston, who hatched a plan to have Kidd commissioned a privateer, permitting him to hunt for pirates and merchant ships of countries unfriendly to England, especially France. Four noble lords, prominent Whigs, invested in the heavily-armed *Adventure Galley* with the expectation of sharing in booty from captured cargos, even the King would skim ten percent off the top.

Kidd recruited 150 sailors with promises of spoils and headed for the Indian Ocean. When he met a fleet of Royal Navy ships off South Africa, British Commodore Thomas Warren announced he would impress at least 30 of Kidd's crewmen, a hated custom of the British Navy. But when Kidd sneaked away overnight, the incensed Warren decided that Kidd was a pirate and spread the word through the oceans, an accusation that followed Kidd the rest of his life. Kidd meanwhile searched fruitlessly for prizes from Madagascar to Somalia and the Red Sea, then east to the coast of India.

Finally, the *Adventure Galley* came upon the 400-ton *Quedagh Merchant* which was carrying a rich cargo and sailing with French papers, making it legitimate prey. But when Kidd learned it was captained by an Englishman and its goods and treasure belonged to a Grand Indian Moghul, he was reluctant to seize the prize. But his surly crew hadn't seen any payoff despite years of cruising and convinced him to take it. He led the merchant ship to Madagascar to sell part of its cargo in the island's shady bazaar. While there, he came across Patrick Culliford, an admitted pirate, whom he planned to capture, but instead most of Kidd's unhappy crew decided Kidd was too wimpy to be a corsair and they joined up with Culliford.

Culliford began chasing lucrative prizes belonging to Indian Muslims and when the Grand Moghul sought revenge, Captain Kidd was included as a target because of his suspect reputation. The English East India Company enjoyed lucrative trade with the Moghul and joined the hunt.

With a sparse crew, Kidd escaped west on the *Quedagh Merchant* around the Cape of Good Hope and eventually to St. Thomas in the Caribbean which Zacks describes as a "tropical Lichtenstein," doing business with all comers. But the governor had heard of Kidd's "piracy" and refused to deal with him. Kidd bought a more seaworthy vessel, the *Saint Antonio*, for 3,000 pieces-of-eight (Spanish dollar coins made of silver), and sailed for New England with 75 pounds of gold, 150 pounds of silver, a pile of jewels, and 29 bales of Persian silk.

Not sure of his reception in Boston, Kidd stopped at Gardiner's Island and asked John Gardiner to bury a treasure chest in Cherry Tree field, still marked to this day, says Zacks. He reunited with Sarah on Block Island and tried to arrange safe entry to Boston to fight the accusations against him.

According to some accounts, the Earl of Bellomont, Governor of Massachusetts, had been involved in commissioning Kidd as a privateer but was anxious to avoid being linked to the "pirate." He fooled Kidd into thinking he'd get a fair hearing, but instead slapped him into solitary confinement. When ordered, John Gardiner brought Kidd's treasure to Bellomont. (The East Hampton Library has a copy of the inventory.) While in prison Kidd had to listen to Cotton Mather preach about ill-gotten gains.

Kidd was put in chains aboard the *Saint Antonio* for a rough winter cruise to London and locked away in the dreadful Newgate Prison. The Tories in power were happy to blame Kidd's supposed crimes on the Whigs who had backed his venture, but the Whigs abandoned him, claiming he's not "our" pirate. Kidd's letters and memoirs in his own defense disappeared at the Admiralty.

He was tried before 400 members of the House of Commons who were more interested in tarring their opponents than in giving him a fair trial. The French papers that would prove he had acted as a privateer in taking the *Quedagh Merchant* also had disappeared into the Admiralty. Some of his former crew who had joined Culliford were hoping for leniency and testified against him. They added the charge of murder for Kidd's whacking a recalcitrant crewman with an "ironbound bucket." He was convicted of piracy and murder and sentenced to death.

Kidd was hanged on May 23, 1701. He prepared for his demise by drinking gallons of rum, but sobered up somewhat when the rope broke and he fell to the ground. Despite a tradition that this was a sign of innocence, he was strung up again. The court ordered his body put into an iron cage, and suspended it at the mouth of the Thames as a warning to pirates. They auctioned off Kidd's gold, silver, and some diamonds and rubies, generating 5,500 pounds, some of which went to an old sailors home. In 1910 an American researcher found the two French papers misfiled at the Board of Trade in London.

The authorities forced Sarah Kidd from the family mansion on Pearl Street in Manhattan and confiscated her other properties. But with legal help she fought back and in 1704 Queen Anne returned her assets. She married a fourth husband, Christopher Rousby, and named one of their offspring, William. Sarah Bradley Cox Oort Kidd Rousby died wealthy in 1744, leaving a sizeable amount to Kidd's grandchildren. Sarah obviously was more successful in fighting British bureaucracy than the incredibly unlucky Captain William Kidd.

✳ ✵ ❋

The Supreme Court Said
Long Island Is a "Peninsula"

On April 29, 1985, the United States Supreme Court under Chief Justice Berger ruled that for legal purposes Long Island is not an "island" but a "peninsula." Just imagine if this decision were carried to its logical conclusions. We'd have "Long Peninsula Sound," "Long Peninsula Railroad" and "Long Peninsula Lighting Company." But that's just the tip of the naming iceberg. Think of the need to change company names and road signs, thousands of maps all over the world, even sports franchises. New York Peninsulars? It boggles the mind.

On his website, Attorney Oscar Michelen says that his old law professor Myles MacDonald was a member of the team representing New York in the case brought by the United States against the 13 states bordering the Atlantic Ocean. The Federal Government conceded that the states had interests in the seabed and subsoil up to three miles from their coastlines, but wanted to affirm its exclusive rights beyond that limit. This made it important to establish the official coastline of each state.

In New York's case, the U.S. argued that the coastline didn't start along the south shore of Long Island, as you'd expect, but along the shores of Westchester County and Connecticut, north of Long Island Sound. This would severely limit New York's rights to its offshore waters. In researching the case Attorney MacDougall discovered that since the East River separating Manhattan from Long Island only became navigable when the Army Corps of Engineers dredged it many years ago, it does not constitute a natural break from the mainland, and voila! Long Island is not an "island" but a "peninsula," making our south shore New York's legal coastline.

The Supreme Court eventually agreed to this position and New York triumphed. To make sense of its decision, the Court had to declare that Long Island Sound is a "juridical bay" whose waters are almost completely enclosed by land and are "state inland waters." Translated from legalese, the Court said that the bay is closed at the line drawn from Montauk Point at the eastern tip of Long Island to Watch Hill Point on the Rhode Island shore, and that the waters of the bay west of the closing line are "internal state waters."

The waters of Block Island Sound east of the line are "territorial waters and high seas." The Court apparently realized the chaos that could occur and said the peninsula designation was only for legal purposes and that we could continue to call our home an island. While New York came out a winner, Rhode Island failed in its rather far-fetched claim that its coastline should run from Montauk Point to Block Island to Point Judith. We surmise that the Feds initiated all this kerfuffle to avoid future disputes with the states regarding rights to fishing, seabed mining, perhaps even offshore wind farms.

In digging through the matter we learned that a 1556 chart of Long Island based on the voyages of Giovanni da Verrazzano shows Long Island as a peninsula named "Flora." The actual chart is in the Brown University Library. We romantics would like to think that mapmaker Giacomo di Gastaldi was immortalizing a girlfriend by that name, but it probably referred to the heavy vegetation on the island (or peninsula) observed by explorers sailing along the coast.

As if being dubbed "Flora" isn't stressful enough, we learned that the citizens of Whidbey Island off the State of Washington seized on the Supreme Court ruling and claimed that their domain, not ours, is the longest island in the contiguous United States. Despite being only 45 miles long, less than half the length of our island, Whidbey Islanders became obsessed with the distinction, advertising it on their website, featuring it in tourist brochures and imprinting it on T-shirts. The *Whidbey Island Historical Museum Newsletter* repeated the claim, and when challenged, said the person who put together the newsletter is "no longer with us," a weasely dodge if ever we heard one. Frankly we never even realized that Long Island is the longest island of the lower 48, but we are New Yorkers and we can't let Washington Staters grab a title that belongs to us.

We take comfort from Dr. Patrick Kennelly, Assistant Professor of Geography at C. W. Post Campus of Long Island University, who said that Long Island is a real island by any definition, and its 118-mile length is more than twice that of Whidbey. We're sure Dr. Kennelly is objective, but really would you expect a scholar who works at Long Island University to say anything else?

According to a 2004 article in the *New York Times*, Professor Michael Bauer of Fordham University joined the battle with Whidbey. He wrote to publishers of a Washington State tourist publication suggesting they correct this"gross inaccuracy" and refer if they must to Whidbey as the "longest juridical-defined island in the lower 48 states per the purpose of applying Article 7 of the Convention on the Territorial Sea and Contiguous Zone, but the second longest in straightforward, geographic terms." We'd like to see them put that on a T-shirt. The publishers responded that they'd keep Dr. Bauer's letter on file but they had just printed a new edition of the *Washington State Handbook,* so nothing could be done for several years. Another evasion by the size-deprived Whidbey Islanders.

We certainly hope New York State and Long Island legislators are alert to the fight and make sure that Whidbey Island doesn't get away with this distortion of the truth. But wait, there may be one small advantage that would come from changing our home to "Long Peninsula." It would stop those New Jersey smart alecks who love to mock us for saying we live on "Long Guy-Land."

The *Pelican II* Took 45 Lives

I t wasn't a perfect fall day. It was cloudy, the wind was kicking up, and there were small craft warnings. But that wasn't going to stop the day-trippers who were intent on fishing, maybe catching the big one. They came out on the LIRR from the City and could walk from the Montauk railroad station to the dock where *Pelican II* was warming its engines. Others drove out from towns on Long Island — families, including a few youngsters, relatives and friends, all looking forward to a day on the water. Captain Eddie Carroll yelled "No more, can't take any more," but by the time the mate cast off her lines and *Pelican II* headed out of Fort Pond Bay, the boat was overloaded with 62 passengers, plus the captain and mate. By mid- afternoon on Saturday, September 1, 1951, 45 of them would be dead.

Pelican II proved again how seemingly minor problems can lead to another and another, and end in disaster, especially at sea, even with land close by. In those days recreational fishermen probably paid around $10 which gave them tight elbow room at the boat rail and an old coffee can of chopped up clams and squid for bait. Most brought their own fishing poles and tackle. At 14 tons, the homely *Pelican II*, a 42-foot "party boat" or "head boat," was just below the tonnage that required meeting Coast Guard regulations and annual inspections.

Pelican II arrived at Frisbie's fishing bank off Ditch Plains at 10 am, according to Van Field in his book *Mayday*. The captain shut down her twin, 100-hp Chrysler engines and began a drift for fish as the people aboard dropped their hooks into the water. Before too long, rough seas made everyone uncomfortable and at around 11:30, Carroll decided to go back inside the Point.

But the engines wouldn't start. He finally got one of the two going, and *Pelican II* made slow headway as a squall line approached, generating a strong northeast wind that blew against an outgoing tide. She rode well enough heading into the wind but when *Pelican II* rounded the Point she turned broadside to 35 mph gusts and 15-foot waves that pushed her over nearly 60 degrees. Then several big waves in a row hit her starboard side and suddenly she capsized, trapping cold and seasick passengers who had sought refuge in the cabin, and throwing those on deck into the rough water.

Though there were plenty of life preservers aboard only one passenger had put one on. Private fishing boats nearby, *Betty Jane* and *Bingo II*, came to the rescue, heaving life jackets to people in the water and pulling 16 of them to safety. An hour later a Coast Guard picket boat arrived and saved one person still clinging to the overturned hull. A CG motor lifeboat that might have aided in the rescue had been called away earlier to search for another vessel in distress. No one bothered to notify the authorities that the other vessel already was safe in port.

Montauk fishing boat captain Frank Mundus secured the overturned hull and later the Coast Guard towed it into Lake Montauk where, according to Jeannette Rattray in *Ship Ashore*, ten bodies were recovered from inside the cabin. For several days, Coast Guard, Navy, and Air Force units searched for bodies along the shore.

William Friedel of East Moriches survived with the help of his 13-year old son, but lost his brother and sister-in-law. Angelo Testa of Patchogue fought desperately against the waves but was unable to save his father.

According to author Van Field, if *Pelican II* had been subject to inspection she probably would have been limited to 20 passengers. It stated that Captain Eddie Carroll, who did not survive, "failed to distribute the weight (passengers) to trim his boat," had not kept track of weather, and came too close to shore when rounding the Point. As invariably happens after a maritime disaster, new safety rules were put in place. "T-boat" regulations which include routine inspections of all vessels for hire carrying more than seven people, and strict limits of passenger capacity went into effect in 1957. ("T-boat" because the rules covering them are laid down in "subchapter T of Title 46 of the Code of Federal Regulation.")

Pelican II was towed to Greenport and hauled at a shipyard where she sat neglected for years, perhaps cursed by the disaster. She gradually fell apart and eventually was cleared away to make room for condominiums.

✳ ✳ ✳

The *Great Eastern*'s Great Misfortunes

How many ships have a rock named after them? There's an underwater crag about a mile east of Montauk Point that has the dubious distinction of being named for the *Great Eastern*, at the time of her launching in 1858 in the Victorian era the biggest ship in the world and considered the prototype of modern ocean liners. She was so large that the shipyard on the River Thames near London launched her sideways, and perhaps in a premonition of her future life, she refused to exit the slipways and hydraulic rams were needed to push her into the river.

Lighthouse historian Henry Osmers says the *Great Eastern*'s engines generated 8,000 horsepower to turn her 56-foot diameter paddlewheels and 24-foot diameter propellers that moved her along at 14 knots. Hedging his bet, marine architect–engineer Isambard Kingdom Brunel designed her with six masts which turned out to be unusable when the engines were working because exhaust from her five funnels might set fire to the sails. Brunel referred to the ship as his Great Babe, and indeed she was — 692 feet long (longer than two football fields), an 83-foot beam and a displacement of 32,000 tons fully loaded. One hundred furnaces steamed ten boilers. Three million rivets, hand-fastened at Scott Russell's Millwall, London shipyard, fabricated unique double hulls of ¾-inch iron, reinforced by ribs every six feet.

Brunel originally intended the ship to carry freight and passengers from Britain to Australia without refueling, but following her reluctant launching, further mishaps piled up. The cost of building Great Babe bankrupted the Eastern Steam Navigation Company and she was sold to the Great Ship Company that refitted her for transatlantic trade.

On her trials in the Atlantic Ocean in 1860, a boiler exploded and killed six crewmen. On a third voyage to Canada, a gale tore off one paddle wheel and smashed the other into pieces. Her 11-inch thick rudder post sheared off and she flopped out of control for several days. Finally engineer Hamilton E. Towle, aboard as a passenger, suggested attaching the rudder to heavy chains which gave the ship some steering. A court later awarded Towle $15,000 under the law of salvage, but because Great Babe's owners were always broke he probably never received a penny.

But getting back to that rock off Montauk, the *Great Eastern* was proceeding from Liverpool to New York City in August 1862, heavily laden with 1,530 passengers and tons of freight aboard. She arrived off Montauk at midnight. The captain feared her deep draft might not make it over the Sandy Hook bar at the entrance to New York Harbor and decided to sail up Long Island Sound to Flushing Bay. At around 2 am, Great Babe hit the rock, known until then as the Northeast Rips. She rumbled and heeled slightly, then blithely proceeded on her way. Inspection later revealed a nine-foot wide, 83-foot long gash in the outer hull, damage much worse than that suffered by the *Titanic*. But being the first ship built with watertight double hulls, *Great Eastern* was repaired and went back to sea within a few months. (Today there are regular demands for such construction, especially for oil tankers.)

The high cost of operation combined with the American Civil War disrupting Atlantic trade, the vessel continued losing money and forced her sale to still another venture, *Great Eastern* Steamship Company which chartered her to the Telegraph Construction and Maintenance Company. Converted in 1865 to her new role, she laid

A model of the *Great Eastern* at the Montauk Lightouse museum.

2,600 miles of transatlantic cable, and between 1866 and 1878 she laid over 30,000 miles of cable, including France to Newfoundland and from Aden on the Red Sea to Bombay.

Subsequent attempts to reintroduce her as an ocean liner failed and she humbly served on the River Mersey as a concert hall and gymnasium, and as a sailing promotion for Lewis Department Store. With no more investors willing to embrace Great Babe, she was scrapped in 1889. One wag remarked it was the first time she made any money. Rumors that workers found a skeleton trapped inside her double hull are considered doubtful.

A couple of years ago, Montauk Lighthouse officials went to an auction in Maine where they bid on an eight-foot long, steel model of *Great Eastern*. It is now on exhibit in the lighthouse museum. So next summer, when you run out of things to do with your weekend guests, take them out to Montauk, climb to the top of the lighthouse, and spin tales about Great Babe and her namesake rock.

The Mystery of the Money Ship

Spanish doubloons, a treasure chest, a sailing ship drifting aimlessly without a soul aboard — it's the stuff of an adventure novel, but it actually happened almost 200 years ago off the coast of Shinnecock. There have been countless shipwrecks along Long Island's south shore, but this was perhaps the strangest, what locals referred to as the wreck of the Money Ship. The unusually rigged ship appeared in the ocean off Southampton after a storm. When the seas calmed and villagers reached her, they found no one aboard, no name or cargo, her sails half furled and furniture and clothing tossed about, as if she had been abandoned in great haste.

The Wrecking Master for the district (yes, there was such a job) took charge, stripped her of sails, rigging and anything else of value, and carted them to a lot on Main Street, Southampton, where they were advertised and sold. On the day of the sale, a buyer found a Spanish dollar wedged in a piece of the rigging which of course prompted closer scrutiny of the entire wreck. No more coins were found until a man strolling the beach picked up a stick and probed into the derelict ship. When he withdrew the stick, another Spanish dollar was wedged into its split end. Again, further searches failed to turn up any more coins and the wreck was sold to be broken up for its planks and timber. This was not uncommon at the time, many a barn and fence on Long Island's south shore came from ships that had piled up on the beach.

Before it was salvaged along came a young whaler, Henry Green, walking the beach. Out of curiosity he climbed aboard the wreck which was partly awash in the surf. Right there on the cabin floor he found a shiny silver dollar. Keeping his find quiet, the next night he and a friend sneaked aboard and searched carefully, but found nothing. Just before leaving the wreck, Green looked up and saw the edge of a coin sticking out of a crack in the low wooden ceiling. Using his jackknife to enlarge the opening, he yanked on a section of the overhead and a shower of dollars came down on his head. He and his pal secretly made many more searches until a hard storm broke up the wreck and scattered more coins into the sand where they were found by treasure hunters now eagerly swarming the beach.

Harry B. Squires reported all of this in the May 1947 issue of the *Long Island Forum*. Among other sources, his report quoted a Mrs. E. P. White of Southampton who claimed that the mystery ship had been sighted earlier off Patchogue during a storm as the crew tried to get to shore in small boats. A big surf capsized the boats and drowned most of the men. When they washed ashore they were discovered to have bags of Spanish dollars strapped to their bodies, no doubt making swimming difficult. The one survivor was the master of the vessel,

John Sloane, who told a convoluted story. He said he had been put in charge of the Spanish ship after it was captured by a Mexican warship. His orders were to take the ship to New York and fit it out as a privateer under the Mexican flag. Apparently unknown to the Mexicans, the Spanish had hidden treasure on the ship which Sloane's crew accidently discovered as the ship was sailing to New York.

When a storm battered the vessel and abandonment loomed, Captain Sloane said he divided the silver money among the crew and packed the more valuable gold and jewels in a big portmanteau which he "intended to account for to the Mexican authorities." But, said Sloane, the portmanteau was lost in abandoning ship so the mystery of the Money Ship remains a mystery to this day.

Apparently the ocean scattered the treasure widely. The *East Hampton Star* of April 15, 1892, reported that "As Fred McCann was crossing the street on Tuesday, he picked up a coin from out of the dust, which proved to be of Spanish coinage, bearing the date of 1740. Fred is now looking up the value of old coins." So when you go for your last ocean swim of the season you might want to keep your eyes peeled and your toes alert for Spanish doubloons buried in the sand, waiting to be discovered.

Local Lighthouses over 100 Years Old

Ben Franklin always spoke clever words on a variety of subjects. Supposedly, returning to port after a storm at sea, he said, "Lighthouses are more helpful than churches." People love lighthouses — to paint them, photograph them, or just admire their towering beauty — perhaps because they are built with the purest of intentions, to guide and reassure. In his fascinating, new book *Brilliant Beacons, A History of the American Lighthouse* Eric Jay Dolin

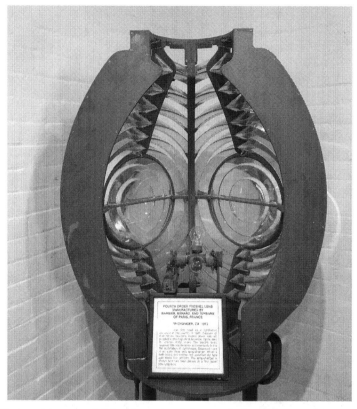

Fresnel lens exhibited at the Montauk Lighthouse Museum.

writes that one of the first issues the infant U.S. Congress took up was whether the federal government or the states should be in charge of lighthouses. There are four lighthouses near Sag Harbor, all different, all well over 100 years old. Three of them still serve as aids to navigation.

Many a Sag Harbor resident whose visitors stayed a day too long has resorted to a trip to Montauk and its famous lighthouse which was authorized by George Washington on April 12, 1792. According to Montauk historian Bryan Penberthy (www.us-lighthouses.com), surveyors sited the beacon on a flat plateau atop a bluff and with great foresight warned that future erosion could threaten the light. (In the

1980s, a major effort led by local resident Georgiana Reid helped slow erosion of the bluff by a system of terracing and planting.)

Congress appropriated $20,000 for construction of the Montauk lighthouse and New York bricklayer John McComb's crew erected an 80-foot tall tower of Connecticut sandstone, walls at the base six feet thick, tapering to three feet at top. A ten-foot tall iron lantern containing thirteen whale oil lamps capped the tower. Ironically, the ship bringing oil went aground at Napeague. First keeper Jacob Hand illuminated the beam in April 1797.

In April 1851, Montauk was upgraded with a first order Fresnel lens. A brilliant Frenchman, Augustin-Jean Fresnel, after experimenting with optics, mainly diffraction and the wave theory of light, developed a huge improvement for lighthouses all over the world. Earlier beams were generated by parabolic reflectors which bounced the light from oil lamps. Fresnel's lens was thinner and lighter than reflectors. It consisted of a central bull's-eye surrounded by concentric rings of triangular prisms which refracted or bent the light into parallel rays, creating a stronger beam that traveled much farther.

According to author Eric Jay Dolin the Fresnel lens originally came in four "orders," or sizes, based on the distance between the lamp and the inner surface of the lens. The first order was the largest and most powerful, used for major seacoast lights, the fourth order, only a foot in diameter, illuminated harbor lights.

Our nearest lighthouse is at Cedar Point, marking the narrow entrance from Gardiner's Bay into Shelter Island Sound. Built in 1839 of granite blocks, it originally sat on a small island guiding ships to Sag Harbor, then one of the busiest ports on the East Coast. Nearly 100 years later the mighty hurricane of 1938 built a sandbar that connected the island to the mainland.

The light was decommissioned and replaced by a simple skeletal tower. At one time Edith Beale, an aunt to Jackie Kennedy Onassis, owned it as a private retreat. In 2002 it was listed on the National

Lantern room of the Cedar Point lighthouse being refurbished.

Register of Historic Places and is now part of Suffolk County Cedar
Point Park. A few years ago its four-ton lantern room was lifted off
and barged to the Sag Harbor Yacht Yard as the first step of renovation by the Long Island Chapter of the U.S. Lighthouse Society.

If you ever have headed north via the Cross-Sound Ferry from
Orient Point you have sailed around the lighthouse known as the
Coffee Pot that was built in 1899 to guide mariners through Plum
Gut. It was designed in the shape of a truncated cone of curved cast
iron plates filled with concrete and resting on rocky Oyster Point
Reef. In 1970 when the Coast Guard declared it too unsafe to service,

it underwent a major renovation with more concrete pumped into the base, and sandblasting and coating. Look closely: the Coffee Pot is about five degrees out of plumb. A fourth-order Fresnel lens flashes white for five seconds.

When you drive between Greenport and Orient, at an open stretch you can see the Long Beach Bar lighthouse off to your right, originally built to guide fishermen into the Peconic Estuary. It is better known as the Bug Light because when first built in 1870 it stood on spindly, insect-like, screw-pile legs driven 10 feet into the sandy bed of Gardiner's Bay. The legs supported a two-story keeper's dwelling as well as the light. In tough winters long ago, ice floes driven by tides threatened the thin support legs, so in 1926 a reinforced concrete foundation was poured for protection.

The light also sparked a romance. Charles Fenton became keeper in May 1887 and two years later, new assistant Charles B. Moore arrived with his daughter Ruth. Ruth and Keeper Fenton had plenty of time to get acquainted and soon decided to marry. They went ashore for the ceremony but returned to the lighthouse for their honeymoon.

The light was decommissioned in 1948 because the sandbar had extended so far beyond its location that it was useless as a channel marker. In 1955 a local group purchased it at auction for $1,710, but on July 4, 1963 fire destroyed the building. North Fork citizens raised $140,000 to build a working replica.

As we said, people love lighthouses. In 1990 it was lit again and a few years later the Coast Guard recognized the second Bug Light as a federal aid to navigation.

Mutiny on the Whaleship *Globe*

The mutiny aboard the whaleship *Globe* that took place in the Pacific Ocean in January 1824 has been called the bloodiest in the history of American whaling. We knew of the grisly events for many years but only recently did I learn that one of the ringleaders and murderers was Silas Payne, said to be "from a respectable family in Sag Harbor." That information came out of *Mutiny On Board The Whaleship Globe* written by William Lay and Cyrus Hussey, survivors of the horrendous incident and its aftermath.

Leader of the mutineers was 22-year old Samuel Comstock, a boatsteerer–harpooner, who a forensic psychologist called "a 19th-century Charles Manson." The *Globe* had sailed out of Martha's Vineyard on December 22, 1822 with a crew of 21, captained by 29-year old Thomas Worth in his first command. In *Demon of the Waters*, author Gregory Gibson wrote that most of the crew were teenagers, "New England mothers sent their sons to kill whales in the Pacific Ocean at an age when modern parents would think twice about letting them have the car for the weekend." And on the *Globe* there would be much more danger than chasing whales.

After success in the whaling grounds off Japan, the ship sailed to the Sandwich (now Hawaiian) Islands for provisioning. Comstock and Payne were recruited in Honolulu, along with five others, to replace men who had jumped ship. (According to Lay and Hussey's narrative, Comstock and Payne weren't in the original crew, while another source says that Comstock did indeed sail on the *Globe* from Martha's Vineyard and had plans right from the start to establish his own tropical kingdom in the South Seas.) Comstock was descended from Rhode Island Quaker stock and was said to have been a wayward youth.

There already was some discontent in the crew from inadequate food, the usual miserable conditions in the forecastle, and the capricious nature of an inexperienced captain. The new arrivals were problems from the start, constantly complaining and sowing discord. The spark that set off the mutiny was Captain Worth's flogging of Joseph Thomas, one of the new hands, for a defiant remark. Seeing increased unrest among the crew, Comstock and four new crew members seized the opportunity for murder and mayhem.

On January 26, 1824, near Fanning Island, 900 miles south of Hawaii, Comstock and three other conspirators, including Silas Payne, crept into Worth's cabin where he was asleep in a hammock. Comstock split the captain's head with an axe, then ordered Payne to strike one of the mates with a boarding knife, an extremely sharp tool about four feet long, used to cut blubber. Mate Gilbert Smith hid for a time and then saved his life by swearing allegiance to Comstock.

The mutineers threw the captain's and mate's bodies overboard. Later when mutineer William Humphries was suspected of plotting to retake the ship, a kangaroo court tried and hanged him from a yard-arm. Fearing that a passing ship could lead to discovering his foul deeds, Comstock intimidated the rest of the crew and threatened that if any lookout failed to report another vessel he would be cooked in try-pots of boiling oil.

After a bloody encounter with natives in the Gilbert Islands, *Globe* sailed to Milli Atoll where Comstock sought to win over the natives by giving them generous gifts. Suspecting that Comstock's plan was to scuttle the *Globe*, kill the crew and make himself king of the island, Payne and three others armed themselves with muskets and shot Comstock. All of this happened within 22 days of the massacre aboard ship.

Payne and his henchman Oliver then made the mistake of sending Gilbert Smith and five others to secure the *Globe* which was on a mooring, but instead they cut the anchor line and set sail, eventually arriving in Valparaiso, Chile, where they were taken into custody by the American consul, Michael Hogan. He sent the *Globe* to Nantucket under a new captain. The whaling merchants there demanded action from the Secretary of the Navy Samuel Southard who gave orders to seek out the mutineers and survivors in the Gilberts.

Meanwhile, back on Milli Atoll, Payne and a couple of other mutineers forced native women into their tents. One morning when the women escaped, Payne caught up with his mistress, beat her and put her in irons. Such outrages soon led the natives to kill the remaining mutineers with spears and stones. Out of nine castaways, only Hussey and Lay survived, protected in benign captivity by native friends. They were rescued in November 1825 by the U.S. Navy Schooner *Dolphin* skippered by Lt. Commander John Percival, known in the Navy as Mad Jack, who had distinguished himself during the War of 1812.

Mad Jack wasn't in a hurry to get back to Chile. He stopped for several months at the Sandwich Islands and Tahiti, and didn't reach Valparaiso until July 1826. It took months for Hussey and Lay to prove their innocence and return home to Nantucket and ordinary life. The horror of the murderous events aboard the *Globe* haunted them for the rest of their lives.

❊ ❋ ❊

A Sailing Treasure Comes Back to Life

Sailors all over the world revere his name. Nathanael Greene Herreshoff has been called the greatest sailboat designer who ever lived. He died in 1938, yet even today, people who know boats are delighted when an authentic craft built in Herreshoff's own Bristol, Rhode Island boat yard becomes available for restoration.

One of these elderly treasures, a Herreshoff 12-½ constructed in 1925, has been donated to the East End Classic Boat Society in Amagansett by Mark T. Hughes of Shelter Island Heights. The boat is named *Tern* and volunteer craftsmen are bringing it back to life. (The reference "12-½" refers to the waterline length of the boat, the overall length is 15 feet 10 inches.) It's a small boat compared to the giant 144-foot cutter Herreshoff designed to defend the America's Cup in 1903, or compared to the grand yachts he built for moguls William Randolph Hearst, J. P. Morgan, several Vanderbilts, and Harry Paine Whitney. Nevertheless the little gaff-rigged 12-½ sloop embodies Herreshoff's genius and the classic beauty of his designs.

The volunteers who come to the boat shop in Amagansett are aware of the heritage that *Tern* represents. Ray Hartjen is the spiritual leader of the shop where I saw several different types of boats in various stages of reconstruction. Pierce Hance, a former Sag Harbor mayor, leads the work on *Tern*. Hance is uncomfortable being called the leader of the crew, he says he only makes suggestions. There's not much chatter among the craftsmen; they go about their jobs carefully, concentrating on getting it right as they bring the boat back to its original form. They're at the boat shop a couple of days a week and already have invested two years of effort on the little vessel.

Many painstaking tasks are underway, such as installing 22 new oak frames that must be steam-shaped to conform to the curves of the hull. They are fastened in place with the guidance of custom-made wedges that precisely space the white-cedar planking. The stem, transom, keel bolts, rub rail, and other key parts are, or will be, newly fashioned. During a recent visit, besides Pierce Hance and Ron Ahlers from North Haven, I met Stuart Close and Richard Davgin from East Hampton, Charlie Fuchs of Montauk, and Leonard Farrauto who lives in Westhampton. They nodded hello and went back to work.

Created in 1914 and an instant success with yachtsmen who wanted a small, easily sailed sloop that could handle the strong winds of Buzzard's Bay, Herreshoff Boat Works built 364 of the craft through 1943. Quincy Adams Yacht Yard later took up the construction and built 51 hulls. Cape Cod Shipbuilding acquired the rights and produced 35 boats in wood, shifting to fiberglass in 1949. You can buy one from them today. With its 735 lb. fixed lead keel the 12-½ easily shoulders through steep chop. An experienced sailor at the yard said

Installing a new rib for a Herreshoff sloop being restored at
the East End Classic Boat Society in Amagansett.

that the boat's "seductive shape and subtle reverse curves enable it to
ghost along in the lightest winds." Builder Doughdish Inc. also makes
the 12-½ in fiberglass. The Shelter Island Yacht Club races a fleet of 59
of them. For purists, you can still buy a wooden version from Artisan
Boatworks of Rockport, Maine.

Steve Nagy, owner of *El Syd*, has devoted years compiling a national registry of the original 364 Herreshoff-built 12-1/2s. Love for
the little sloop inspires great loyalty in its owners. Norman Tate says
his *Dervish III* is "just as much a part of me as an arm and a leg." Well-
known yacht designer Chuck Paine said of his *Petunia* "I would not
part with it at any price except by divine intervention."

Nathanael Greene Herreshoff was born in 1848 in Bristol, Rhode
Island. After he graduated from MIT with a degree in mechanical

A Herreshoff sloop "ghosts" along in light wind.

engineering, he and his brother John Brown formed the Herreshoff Manufacturing Company which eventually grew to over 400 employees. J. B. negotiated with wealthy clients while Nathanael built hundreds of beautiful designs. Some of Herreshoff's best knpwn creations include *Reliance*, the largest America's Cup boat ever built, the first U.S. Navy torpedo boats, the *Alerion 26, Fishers Island 31*, and the famous one-design racers of the New York Yacht Club.

His most legendary designs were eight successful defenders of the Americas Cup in the period from 1893 to 1934. The Herreshoff Marine Museum in Bristol encompasses the old Herreshoff homestead, six buildings of the former boat works, and a number of its beautiful vessels. One of the museum's rooms holds hundreds of models Nathanael Greene Herreshoff used to imagine his designs. To this day he is referred to as the "Wizard of Bristol."

5

Business Enterprise

Long Island Journalism: Born in Sag Harbor

Sag Harbor should be proud — Frothingham's *Long-Island Herald*, published in the village from 1791 to 1798, was the first, and during its run, the only newspaper on Long Island. According to Steven Coleman, writing in the *Long Island Historical Journal* (*LIHJ*), the *Herald*'s owner, Henry Packer Dering, and its printer–editor David Frothingham, deserve a prominent place in the history of American journalism.

A country newspaper editor in those years lifted material from larger papers and combined it with local news and letters. Printed on a single sheet and folded into four pages, the first few pages of the *Herald* were devoted to foreign, domestic, and local news. Page four featured ads, poetry, and anecdotes. Frothingham liked to inject colorful items, such as this opinion of King George III of England: "…former kings of England usually kept fools for the amusement of themselves and their ministers. Being a rigid economist, it is suspected that his present majesty is determined to spare the drained purses of his subjects by playing that part himself."

Battles between the two political parties in the infant United States (no, nothing has changed) gave the *Herald* plenty to talk about. Alexander Hamilton led the Federalists who were committed to a fiscally sound, central government, a national bank, and better relations with England. Thomas Jefferson and James Madison led the Republicans who favored a decentralized, agrarian republic and denounced a national bank. They resented the British monarchy and favored France as a counterbalance. These icons of American history were also very human politicians and fought each other strenuously, rewarding supporters with patronage and taking revenge on opponents.

Back then, newspapers boldly supported their owners' political positions. According to the *LIHJ* article, Dering initially was a Federalist and for that reason was appointed by Alexander Hamilton, a staunch Federalist and Secretary of the Treasury, to the influential position of Customs Collector when Sag Harbor became an official Port of Entry. The appointment launched Dering's career in government and trade, and pointed towards another coveted post, Sag Harbor postmaster. Dering's fingers were in every pie. Besides his two official positions, he acquired shares in the town wharf, partnered with John Fordham in the village's general store, was clerk to the town trustees, a trustee of the Presbyterian Church, and a member of the public school committee.

Dering controlled the *Herald*'s political direction and he and Frothingham began moving their allegiance from the Federalists towards the Republicans. Dering's family had fled to Connecticut during the Revolutionary War, and he hated the British for plundering Long Island. He also admired Republican Thomas Jefferson's "concept of the yeoman farmer as a bulwark of the new Republic." In the summer of 1791, the *Herald* printed the first installment of Thomas Paine's *The Rights of Man* which took a sharp jab at England. All of this put Dering at odds with Hamilton and foreshadowed the deeper divide between Republicans and Federalists.

A few years later, seeking to resolve provocations by the Royal Navy, U.S. officials signed the Jay Treaty with Britain which angered both the French and Henry Packer Dering. Referring to the treaty, Dering editorialized, "Does there exist an independent American so lost to all recollection of the past conduct of the British government?"

Elected in 1796 to succeed George Washington, Federalist John Adams began firing Republicans from customs and postal jobs. Dering survived because Adams needed his influence in Suffolk County for what turned out to be Adams's unsuccessful run for a second presidential term in the 1800 election. Probably to avoid conflict with President Adams and Treasury Secretary Hamilton, Dering shut down the *Herald* that year. Frothingham left Sag Harbor and went to work for the *New York Daily Argus* which promoted competition for Hamilton's Bank of New York. Hamilton got his revenge by arresting Frothingham for libel on another matter and he was tried and sent to prison for four months.

Dering became a staunch Republican and once Jefferson's party took control in 1800, Dering published a succession of political papers in Sag Harbor — the *Suffolk County Herald*, the *Suffolk Gazette*, and the *Suffolk County Recorder*. He might only have stopped because he was running out of names. He continued as Collector of the Port and postmaster until his death in 1822. You can visit Sag Harbor's Customs House where Dering lived during those formative years of our country, and where he and his wife Anna Fosdick raised nine children. It provides an intimate look at the lifestyle of this vital man.

Steamboats Were Vital in Early America

When the steamboat *Shinnecock* built by the Montauk Steamboat Company left Pier 13 on the East River on almost any morning in the 1890s, office workers hurrying to their jobs on Wall Street stopped and stared in wonder at the "smoke and clatter and pounding paddles." Her coal-fired steam engines generated 2,500 horsepower to turn giant, side paddle-wheels that would propel her up to 17 mph and power her through treacherous Hell Gate into Long Island Sound.

Three decks topped by a giant black funnel accommodated 84 staterooms in her 250-foot length. After a stop at Greenport, the *Shinnecock* would arrive at Sag Harbor at 4 o'clock that afternoon and disembark hundreds of passengers onto Long wharf. From there they walked to the American Hotel and country inns, or took stages to Bridgehampton and East Hampton. The next morning the *Shinnecock* boarded new passengers and returned to Manhattan. Full fare was two dollars.

By the mid-19th century, the nation was bursting at the seams with immigrants, entrepreneurs, and adventurers who would thrust the young country into a prominent place in the world. With a still crude road system inadequate for land travel, steamboats on waterways all over the country provided low freight rates and faster transport. By 1830 eighty steamboats sailed the Hudson River and Long Island Sound. They rivaled ocean liners in bulk and magnificence. Their origins went back to John Fitch in 1787 and Robert Fulton in 1807.

In 1855, an advertisement in the *New York Times* announced a "new route" for Greenport and Sag Harbor.

> The splendid steamer, *Island Belle*, Capt. J. Post, Jr., will leave New York from Catherine Market-slip for Sag Harbor, on Tuesday, Thursday, and Saturday at 11 am. Returning will leave Sag Harbor on Monday, Wednesday, and Friday at 10 am, landing at Greenport, Orient Point, and Northport both ways. Fare to and from Sag Harbor, Greenport, and Orient Point $1.50, Northport 50 cents. Freight taken at reasonable rates, payable on delivery of the goods.

Interior decor of the Long Island Sound steamers varied widely but many were quite ornate. The *Bristol* steamboat of the Fall River Line, was described as a

> ...floating palace. In the main saloon, ladies saloon, and social hall, may be seen very delightful specimens of good taste in the selection of the new velvet carpets, rugs, mats, silk curtains, lace curtains.... The whole of the furniture in the grand saloon and ladies saloon is covered in plum-colored velvet, while that of the social hall is done in velvet and rep.

Another glowing description referred to "gilt-edged spittoons," apparently a mark of elegance.

Business wasn't limited to New York City. A commerce report by Congress included the data that in 1866 two smaller steamboats made over 200 trips between New London and Sag Harbor carrying some 10,000 passengers. The *Long Island Forum*, a valuable source of local history, wrote of the steamboat *Sunshine* running between Sag Harbor and Hartford in 1887, and in earlier years between Sag Harbor, Greenport, Shelter Island ,and New London, making a round trip daily.

By the early 20th century, wood-hulled steamboats gave way to steel hulls and used coal instead of wood to fire high-pressure boilers. Coal figured in an accident on Long Wharf in July, 1908. The *Brooklyn Times* reported

> While backing a train of two coal cars down on Long Wharf... Engine 23 which runs between this place [Sag Harbor] and Bridgehampton, undermined the tracks which...toppled into the bay...Engineer Joseph Smith stuck to his post and shut off the controlling lever and hung on for life as the engine fell. The cow-catcher, forward trucks and boiler were submerged.

We presume Long Wharf was subsequently reinforced.

As any sailor will tell you, if you go to sea often enough, you inevitably will face a crisis. In January 1840 the 120-foot paddle-wheeler *Lexington*, built by Cornelius Vanderbilt, left New York for Stonington, Connecticut, on a bitterly cold day. Aboard were 115 passengers and a cargo of bales of cotton loaded around the smokestack casing. Soon after she entered Long Island Sound, encountering strong wind and heavy seas, fire broke out among the bales of cotton and couldn't be contained. Captain George Child headed for the north shore of Long Island, hoping to beach the vessel, but the rudder lines burned through and the ship went out of control. Passengers jumped overboard to escape the flames but succumbed in the icy water. Only four people survived the disaster, one of them Second Mate David Crowley who dug into the center of a cotton bale and floated ashore 48 hours later.

A greater tragedy struck in June of 1904 when the 235-foot *General Slocum* of the Knickerbocker Steamship Company headed up the East River on a chartered trip to Eaton's Neck near Huntington. She carried 1,342 passengers, mostly women and children from a German-American Lutheran Church who looked forward to a pleasant sail and a picnic ashore. As she passed 90th Street, fire broke out in the paint room, possibly from a cigarette, and spread quickly. Rotten fire hoses, aged life preservers, and wired-in-place lifeboats added to the terror. She sank near North Brother Island just off the Bronx with a loss of 1,021 people, the worst single disaster in New York City until 9/11, over a hundred years later. As a result, Federal and State governments enacted tough regulations for ship safety equipment. Her captain was convicted of negligence and served three-and-a-half years in Sing Sing.

The Montauk Steamboat Company mentioned earlier became part of the Long Island Railroad in 1899, after the two had competed for business between New York City and Eastern Long Island and beyond. Besides the *Shinnecock*, the company ran the steamboats *Montauk, Orient,* and *Nantasket* and established daily service from New York.

One passenger in those steamboat days wrote that "the old whaling town [that's us] is my favorite place on Long Island...even if it gets more foo-foo all the time."

A Bootlegger's Paradise

When the 18th Amendment to the Constitution of the United States was ratified on January 29, 1919, Prohibition became the law of the land. Congressman Andrew J. Volstead, backed by evangelicals and reformers, defined intoxicating liquors as any beverage containing more than one-half of one percent alcohol. There's more alcohol than that in hair tonic. The effects on the country were devastating — organized crime expanded to dominate the distribution of illegal liquor, police were often corrupted by payoffs, disrespect for the law grew, and consumption of alcohol actually increased during the 13 years Prohibition was in effect.

Many years ago, the *Sag Harbor Express* reported that during those days liquor was available "under the counter" to anyone who wanted it. "There are old timers in Sag Harbor who can recall speakeasies in North Haven, Sag Harbor, and East Hampton." A few entrepreneurs made their own hootch but the best came from overseas through Nova Scotia, Bermuda, Canada, and the West Indies. Ocean-going supply vessels loaded with hundreds of cases of liquor would lie in a "row" three miles off Long Island, just beyond U.S. jurisdiction, and await local "rumrunners" in small, fast boats who would take aboard whatever they could carry and head for the East End's bays and coves.

The booze would be hidden until it was loaded onto trucks for the run to Manhattan and its numerous speakeasies. Later, the international limit was pushed out to 12 miles which called for faster, bigger speedboats. Some of them, said George Finkenor, writer of the *Express* article, were powered by surplus Liberty aircraft engines from World War I. Supposedly a big name in rum running was Captain Bill McCoy who was not connected with any syndicate and who became known for handling the best, uncut booze. Liquor from this "honest crook" was considered "the real McCoy."

In August 1923, wrote Dorothy Zaykowski in her definitive book *Sag Harbor: An American Beauty*, agents raided a Noyac home and discovered 119 cases of liquor originating from Scotland and the Bahamas. No one was home to arrest. In 1927, a *Saturday Evening Post* writer came to Sag Harbor to report on rum running activities. The proprietor of the American Hotel at the time told him that things were quiet now but a year ago the village was busy with motorboats bringing liquor in from the "row," and trucks leaving for Manhattan in the middle of the night.

In his book *The Dark Side of Camelot*, well-known investigative reporter Seymour M. Hersh wrote that Peter Maas, another prize-winning journalist, was told by Mafia boss Frank Costello that he and Joseph Kennedy had been partners in bootlegging. In a 1983 memoir *A Man of Honor*, another Mafia chieftain, Joe Bonanno, said the same thing, quoting Costello that he would sometimes go to Sag Harbor in the summer. "This was one of the coves, so I was told, that the Kennedy people used to transport whisky during Prohibition."

In April 1923 under a front page headline "Harbor Man Held in Rum Raid," the *Express* reported that officers raided the premises of one Krupinsky on Atlantic Avenue. The officers seized a boiler and "several gallons of alleged illegal intoxicants and mash.... A report that during the raid the gutters of Goat Alley were flowing with hootch...could not be authenticated."

An article in the *Southampton Press* reporting on a library talk by village old-timers said local farm fields supplied corn, potatoes, and rye that crude distilleries could turn into liquor. When the Feds raided a large still just north of Bridgehampton, they caught two of its operators, but two others "jumped out the window and ran into the woods to Noyac." The story-tellers said that locals could make more money transporting liquor than distilling it since they generally had faster boats than the government and knew all the inlets and harbors. One fellow installed heavy springs in his Chrysler Roadster and packed in 10 cases, worth $5 each at his Brooklyn destination. He was stopped by revenue agents on Montauk Highway but he had hidden the liquor underneath crates of cauliflower and they let him go.

On February 16, 1930 the *New York Times* ran a lengthy article describing two incidents in which the Coast Guard shot at suspected rum runners. "Early in the week, shots had been fired from the Coast Guard Cutters *Eagle* and *Niniha* at East Hampton when residents of the vicinity approached the water line where liquor from a stranded run runner had been jettisoned." Among those fired on were Sag Harbor men Cecil C. Wyen, William Petty, Frederich Budd, and Romeo Bozze.

In another incident, James Hildreth of Southampton complained to the Suffolk County District Attorney that he and a party of men and women were returning around 3:30 am from a Masonic Dinner–Dance at the Fort Pond Restaurant in Montauk. Near Napeague Beach, pistol shots whizzed by their cars. They screeched to a stop and were surrounded by Coast Guardsmen who apologized and asked them to forget the incident.

George Finkenor tells about the ocean going vessel *Beatrice Kay* which was boarded by Coast Guardsmen near Cedar Point but was found to be loaded only with fish and ice. The captain said he was putting into Sag Harbor for repairs. The Coast Guard skipper doubted the alibi and escorted the ship to New London where they almost tore it apart before discovering 1,600 sacks of Meadville Pure Rye Whisky. A judge found the crew not guilty, stating the Coast Guard had no right to board the *Beatrice Kay* without a search warrant since the ship was the home of the crewmen and therefore inviolate.

Prohibition helped Sag Harbor prosper during the early years of the Depression and its repeal in 1933 was partly to blame for sending the village into a long funk. Stories about those days abound and it's impossible to tell which ones are accurate, but it was another colorful chapter in the history of the old whaling village.

"Wine Is Proof God Loves Us"

We were pleased when Ben Franklin stated, "Wine is proof that God loves us and wants us to be happy." At the same time we've too often been intimidated by wine snobs who pontificate, "It's a naïve domestic burgundy, without any breeding, but I think you'll be amused by its presumption." Roman Roth, winemaker and technical director at Wölffer Estates, has no patience with such pretense and is definitely on the side of Old Ben. While more than able to discuss the science and art of his trade, his number one aim is to make wines that are "food friendly," graceful complements of good dining.

The personable Roth has a passion for his work and wouldn't think of trading it for any other pursuit, but when questioned, he points out the many pitfalls in the path of producing good wine, year after year. Roth presides over 50 acres of vineyard in Sagaponack and 25 more acres on the North Fork growing grapes for Rosés, Chardonnays, Sparkling Wines, Merlots, and Rieslings that are highly respected, not only by grape lovers but also by experts in the sophisticated world of wine.

He explains that Wölffer is a "traditional" winery in the sense that he isn't required to meet a marketing idea of what will be an easy sell, but is free to follow the dictates of the vines, using his knowledge and intuition to achieve the best wine from a particular plot. Roth says Rosés are exploding in popularity, with Wölffer's popular dry version helping to make it trendy and fun to drink. He predicts that Wölffer Chardonnay, closer to Burgundy-style than California, will give that wine a new boost in popularity. "Normally you would have to pick earlier to emulate European producers, but Long Island's climate enables us to pick later for more ripeness and character." He claims their White Horse Label Chardonnays are the equal of the best in the world.

Probably few people in the business have accumulated Roth's depth of training and experience. He grew up in a winemaking family in

Rottweil, Germany, and in 1982, as a teenager, began a three-year, hands-on apprenticeship in the Oberrotweil Wine Cooperative, combined with book study at Berufsfachschule in Heilbron. In 1986 he traveled to Carneros, California, to work at Saintsbury Estate, known for its Pinot Noirs and Chardonnays.

The next stop in his world-wide wine education was at Australia's Rosemount Estate. He then returned to Germany to Winzerkeller Wieslock in Baden where the winery won awards for Rieslings, Pinot Noirs, and Methode Champenoises. In 1992 Roth received his Master Winemaker and Cellar Master degrees from the College of Oenology and Viticulture in Weinsberg, a town that has produced wine since the 13th century, so they probably know something about the grape.

The dream of the young winemaker came true when he joined the start-up Sagpond Vineyards in the Hamptons, later renamed Wölffer Estates, and played an important role in the emerging Long Island wine region. In 2003 the East End Food and Wine Awards, judged by the American Sommelier Society, named him Winemaker of the Year in recognition of the "excellence of his wines and his contribution to quality winemaking on the Island." Along the way, Christian Wölffer, who founded the business, allowed Roth to create his own label which enjoys the inevitable brand name, The Grapes of Roth, and has become highly respected.

The woes that can beset a vineyard are almost biblical. Before you even plant, you must mull over soil type and chemistry, fertility and drainage, topography, sun exposure, and aeration. Of course you can't control the weather and each weather condition affects vineyards in different ways. The winemaker and the vineyard manager who tends the vines must adjust constantly to achieve consistent quality in both good and bad weather years. The leaf canopy of the vines must be closely controlled to welcome sun and air and retard fungus. Roth says quality winemaking requires close teamwork, especially with his Vineyard Manager Richie Pisacano whom he describes as a perfectionist.

Wölffer wine comes out of these beautiful vineyards.

The devil is in the details at every stage of winemaking. The command decision of when to pick, the "crossroad," is crucial, a scientific and instinctive judgment of ripeness, sugar content, acidity, berry taste, and tannins. During the fermentation stage, Roth follows an old tradition of letting the wine lie in barrels with "fine lees" (yeast and cells of grape skins) for up to eight months, rather than taking the lees away too soon and losing enhancement of the final product. Timing the separation is another crucial and intuitive decision. Balance is a word Roth uses frequently. Besides his goal of food friendliness, Roth aims for graceful ageing and authenticity, meaning a wine that reflects the best characteristics of its region in an elegant balance of structure, flavor, and body.

In their classic reference, *The Taste of Wine*, Emile Peynaud and Jacque Blouin describe the challenge of harmoniously blending some twenty different flavor constituents "present in quantities measured in grams or fractions of grams per liter. They constitute the bricks and mortar of a wine, its framework…." No wonder there are so many bad wines on the market, yet even more wonder that there are many bottles of high quality.

Next time you dream of owning a vineyard, getting away from the daily push and pull of business, sitting peacefully and gazing over the grapes ripening in the sun, think it over. Hidden in that sunny vineyard lurk dozens of complicated decisions you can't begin to imagine. Better to kick back, uncork a Chardonnay or Merlot and let Roman Roth worry about the vicissitudes of winemaking.

Windmills in Early Sag Harbor

If we thought about them at all, we city kids imagined that the charming windmills on the East End were built for the delight of tourists. Maybe we eventually realized that bread and pasta and pizza dough starts with flour, and those strange-looking towers had something to do with it. Ancient peoples ground grain by hand thousands of years ago, before the invention of the wheel, and benefitted from the carbs and protein in the flour they produced. In the 12th century, windmills, perhaps originating in China (didn't everything?), ground wheat in England. The windmills of the East End descended from these early structures and, entirely non-polluting, using the free energy of the wind, were far ahead of today's efforts to clean up the environment. In 1780 four windmills operated in Sag Harbor. (The structure at Long Wharf wasn't one of them, it was built as a tourist information center.)

Windmills on Long Island developed into wooden-walled towers, usually octagonal, with sloping sides. The most common colonial

Windmill at the base of Long Wharf offers village information.

mills were called "smock" mills after the drape shape of workmen's garb. The earliest smock mill was built on Gardiner's Island in 1795. Eleven wind-powered grist mills ("grist" refers to grain or ground grain), still grace the East End, the largest group of such mills in the United States.

In 1820, Lester Beebe, a retired whaling captain looking for an easier line of work, financed an innovative mill on Sherry Hill in Sag Harbor. It was the last one erected on eastern Long Island and the first to use cast iron gearing. Until then, all inner workings, including gears, were fashioned from wood. The Beebe mill sported a fantail that automatically rotated the windmill's cap on greased metal rings, keeping the sails turned into the wind. Besides grinding flour, meal and feed, the tall Beebe mill raised a flag to alert everyone in the village when a whaling ship was returning from a long voyage. Many years ago the Beebe mill was moved to Bridgehampton.

An existing windmill in Water Mill, built earlier without a fantail, features a tail pole extending from the cap, resting on a cartwheel and relying on man or beast power to turn the cap into the wind. Built on North Haven in 1800, James Corwith moved it with the help of 12 yoke of oxen to Water Mill in 1814. It ground wheat into flour for over 80 years.

The inside of a smock mill looks like the inside of a giant clock. Long timbers at each of the eight corners of the building taper inward toward the top to accommodate the slight angle of the sail assembly. By means of a large gear, the sails directed the force of the wind to turn a center shaft inside the tower. Another gear called the spur wheel at the bottom of the shaft turned a grinding stone over a stationary bed stone, no doubt with much rumbling and grumbling. The force needed to rotate the center shaft and heavy grinding stone testifies to the strength of the inner workings and the power of the wind caught by those flimsy-looking sails. An engineer calculated that in a full gale, a windmill could generate 50 hp.

To early settlers windmills were critical to supplying the community's food needs and contributing to its economy. One entrepreneurial miller advertised in the Sag Harbor *Republican Watchman* in March of 1879 "…doing good work on all kinds of grain, wheat a specialty. I will guarantee a large percentage of fine flour from good wheat: am also prepared to grind very fast and very fine."

The flat topography of Long Island and steady winds from the bays and ocean made windmills perfect for the region. To start the process, millers would carry bags of grain up steep, spiral steps to the top floor (they must have been built like NFL linemen), and poured the grain into wooden chutes that fed below into a center hole in the moving grindstone. As the flour ground finer and finer, it migrated to the edge of the bed stone and into a hopper where it was sifted and bagged. Each farmer's grain was loaded into his own bag of closely woven homespun linen and sold or brought back to the farmstead where it was baked into bread by hard-working colonial wives.

City kids can learn more by going to: *Windmills on Long Island* by Robert Hefner, *Windmills and Water Mills of Long Island* by Sr. Ann Francis Pulling, *The Windmill* by William Thompson, and *The Mills of Long Island* by Rex Wailes.

Torpedoes in Sag Harbor?

As the whaling industry faded away in the latter half of the 19th century, beaten down by the discovery of underground oil and the depletion of whale fisheries, Sag Harbor lost thousands of jobs and scrambled to find employment for its citizens. An unexpected and unusual source of work for the old whaling village came from the First World War which broke out in 1914. For five years during the conflict, E. W. Bliss Company tested U.S. Navy torpedoes in Noyac Bay and Gardiner's Bay, and based its support operations in Sag Harbor. To handle the work, the company leased Long Wharf from the LIRR which owned it at the time, and reinforced it with concrete to handle heavy equipment. The railroad built spurs along the wharf to facilitate loading torpedoes onto test ships. Some 125 men earning sizeable paychecks worked directly on testing, while scores of Sag Harbor merchants, craftsmen, and boatmen benefitted from Navy activities during those tight economic times.

(Most of this information came from an article in the *Lewiston Saturday Journal* of February 10,1916, published in Lewiston, Maine.

There was no byline and it's a puzzle why their reporter was in Sag Harbor in February.)

Most of us are familiar with the effective use of torpedoes by German U-boats in the Second World War, but it may be a little surprising that the same tactics were used in the First World War as German subs tried to stop cargo vessels from carrying supplies to England. Originally referred to as "fish" or "mines," early torpedoes go all the way back to the War of 1812 when a Sag Harbor patriot tried to attack a British Naval ship in Gardiner's Bay.

During the years of World War I, E. W. Bliss Company built Whitehead torpedoes in its plant in Brooklyn, then boxed vital components and shipped them on the LIRR to Sag Harbor. Here, Bliss assembled the parts and carried out rigid tests devised by the Ordnance Bureau of the U.S. Navy under the supervision of a Naval officer.

A structure built on Long Wharf held powerful compressors that injected air under great pressure into the torpedo air flasks. A combination of fulminate, denatured alcohol, superheated air and steam sped the undersea weapon up to 33 knots (almost 40 mph). During five years of this precarious work, there were no serious injuries though one torpedo went wild and knocked a hole in a schooner.

Initially Bliss tested the torpedoes in Noyac Bay at a range of 800 yards, then shifted to Gardiners Bay where the range increased to 12,500 yards, or a little over seven miles. Along the way the Whitehead torpedo was replaced by the Bliss–Leavitt model invented by Frank W. Leavitt of Smithtown, Long Island. World-famous inventor Thomas Alva Edison headed the Naval Consulting Board during World War I and came to Sag Harbor to observe the tests.

As work on testing progressed, Bliss assembled a fleet of 15 support vessels. An old tug named *Agnes* was superseded by the gunboats *Sarah Thorpe* and the *Eliphalet Bliss*. Later, Bath Iron Works in Maine (perhaps that's what brought the Lewiston reporter here) built a specially designed vessel to support longer range tests on Gardiner's Bay.

Named the *Emblane*, it was 130 feet long, 31 feet in the beam and displaced 308 tons. Berthed in Sag Harbor, it loaded 12 to 18 torpedoes at Long Wharf and sailed out each day to moorings in Gardiner's Bay where it fired the test weapons, then returned in the evening. In order to be accepted, each torpedo had to make three perfect hits including two angle shots. The Lewiston newspaper doesn't describe how the torpedoes were retrieved but another source mentions capturing them in fish nets. Captain Fred Youngs commanded the *Emblane*. Youngs had worked previously for the Montauk Steamboat Company and skippered a steamer between New York, Greenport, and Sag Harbor.

Unlike the Germans, the U.S. Navy didn't have many reasons to use torpedoes in World War I and the Bliss–Leavitt models were retired in 1922. It's ironic that in the early days of World War II, American submariners were frustrated by malfunctioning torpedoes despite the fact they supposedly were more sophisticated than the ones tested years earlier in Sag Harbor. It took nearly 18 months before completely reliable torpedoes were supplied to U.S. submarines in the Pacific.

✳ ✳ ✳

President Madison's Suit

When President James Madison ordered a tailored suit to wear to a White House reception on New Year's Day, 1811, he had no idea that his simple request eventually would involve East End luminaries Dr. Ebenezer Sage of Sag Harbor, General Sylvester Dering of Shelter Island, and John Lion Gardiner, owner of Gardiner's Island. Or that the wool from merino sheep that sailed from Spain to Sag Harbor would become a popular material for men's suits in the young United States.

Dr. Sage was a congressman representing Suffolk in the juvenile American government. He was also an entrepreneur and was the source in Washington D.C. for homespun cloth, some of which his friend John Lion Gardiner supplied from a flock of sheep he kept on his island. On December 24th, 1810, Sage explained to Gardiner that President Madison's tailor had asked Sage for fabric to make a new suit for the president. Madison wanted to wear the suit to the January 1st reception at the Capital that would be attended by more than a thousand citizens scoffing punch, wine, cakes and sweetmeats. But Sage said he only had on hand very coarse homespun which would not do for the chief executive.

The fabric also had to be black. Sage complained that he had received no black fabric from Gardiner, and that he would have to use seven yards of fine black Cassimere (presumably what we today call "cashmere") sent to him by General Sylvester Dering of Shelter Island. Dering raised cashmere goats on a farm with his brother Henry Packer Dering. (As you know, Henry was also collector of the port and postmaster of Sag Harbor — the Dering boys were into everything.) Apparently the Derings and Gardiner competed for Dr. Sage's Washington business.

Malcolm Willey told this story in the October 1949 issue of *Long Island Forum*. Today Dr. Sage would be considered a marketing guru. He was aware that some Congressmen were talking about importing merino sheep, a step that would free the United States from dependence on fine woolens from England. For years the export of merino sheep from Spain had been forbidden, but the Napoleonic wars broke that restriction. Sage sensed that the president's request was an opportunity to promote business for his East End constituents, and take a jab at England at the same time. "I told the tailor that while he was measuring the President he should hint that if he wanted a suit for New Year, 1812, a year later, I would bring him wool from full-blooded merino sheep that should do honor to American manufacturers." If the President took up the offer, Dr. Sage wrote, "I think my friend

Henry P. Dering and his brother the General would exert themselves and shear the old Buck at least twice in the season."

The arrival of these animals from Spain to New York State, including Long Island, encouraged textile production here, prompting the birth of a new industry. A merino craze developed early in the 1800s with the Dering brothers, and we presume Gardiner too, whooping it up. It is estimated that between April 1810 and August 1811, nearly 20,000 merino sheep cruised to the United States, a number of them landing on the east end.

In the same year a Gardiner relative in New York City advised his cousin John Gardiner that it was a good time to buy merino ewes and rams. "The sheep is much larger than our common sheep," he wrote, "...It is called Fresan Ram — Fresan being a place in the interior of Africa from whence they are originally obtained."

The resulting merino mania made clear what Dr. Sage had in mind when he offered a suit to the President made of full blooded merino wool "that should do honor to American manufacturers." Author Willey doesn't say if Madison actually ever donned a suit made from merino wool sheared in Sag Harbor. Sage probably didn't care, his plan to support business for his constituents, and maybe for himself, while needling the British, made his venture a success.

Even today, over 200 years later, merino wool is considered one of the finest fabrics for clothing, especially for outdoor activities where warmth, softness and wicking qualities are in demand. The local merino boom didn't last long, whether because of growth of the whaling industry early in the 1800s which promised more immediate profits, or because of competition from western States and Australia. Production of merino wool on Long Island dwindled away and today you would be hard-pressed to find a Fresan Ram anywhere in the Hamptons.

※ ✳ ✳

Howard Pickerell,
Patron Saint of Peconic Oysters

I n bygone days, we always had a sticky jar of English marmalade in
the back of the kitchen cabinet that was labeled in ornate type, "By
appointment to Her Majesty the Queen." On that basis it would
be fair for Howard Pickerell to stamp his oysters, "By appointment
to the American Hotel." When asked about the Pickerell oysters featured on his menu, Ted Conklin, proprietor of Sag Harbor's landmark
hostelry, said "Howard Pickerell is the patron saint of Peconic Bay
oysters. We love him." The manager at the Main Street hotel and restaurant claims there are no better oysters, that they have a "friendly"
taste, even aphrodisiac powers "if you believe in such a thing."

One reason for such gustatory acclaim is the freshness of the bi-
valves that Pickerell supplies. "They call me in the morning," says
Howard. "I go out on Little Peconic Bay, select oysters that are at their
peak, and deliver them the same day." It's not surprising that Pickerell
works ten and twelve hour shifts during the busy season. He grows
the oysters from an infant stage, called spat, coddles them in plastic
mesh cages he refers to as "bags," then regularly cleans and tends
them until they're ready for harvesting. Now and then he vigorously
shakes the bags to break off the oysters' feather edges to make them
fatter.

With diligent care, Pickerell's oysters reach marketable maturity in
18 months rather than the normal two or three years. Each bag that
Howard tends may hold 250 oysters at various stages of growth.

To keep up with demand from the American Hotel and other
top restaurants like Pierre's in Bridgehampton and Coast Grille in
Noyac, Howard purchases 300,000 spat every year from hatcheries in
Southold and Islip. Nature is cruel and a large percent of the spat do not
survive, succumbing to predators, smothering or freezing. (Howard's
son, Chris, is a marine biologist currently working with Cornell to

promote growth of eel grass which provides a natural nursery for many kinds of shellfish.)

Even healthy, adolescent oysters can be killed by oyster drills, tiny predatory sea snails that, second to sea stars or star fish, are the bane of oystering.

Bayman and oyster master Howard Pickerell.

Only an inch or so long, they latch on and bore a neat, round hole in the shells of young oysters and consume them. In 2010 Howard says he removed as many as 50 drills every day from his string of bags. According to Biomes Marine Biology Center, oyster drills and sea stars don't like low salinity water, and, perhaps due to heavy rains that brought an abundance of fresh water to the bays, the problem wasn't as great in 2011.

Howard says Little Peconic Bay's ideal growing conditions encourage oysters to mature more rapidly. The waters are rich with nutrients for them to feed on. Fifty years ago, dredge boats from Connecticut brought young oysters to the Peconics to help them grow faster, like sending the kids to summer camp. In 2010 several streaks of red tide crept into the bay, but they didn't affect Howard's crop. Strangely, even though oysters thrive and grow faster in the bay, they don't reproduce there which is why hatcheries are needed to induce spawning. Howard worries that population growth and building along the shore has increased run-off of toxins into the bays, and he strongly supports efforts to monitor and protect the Peconic Estuary.

Some years ago Pickerell underwent a quintuple bypass operation at St. Francis Hospital in Port Washington. They told him he couldn't leave the hospital until he was able to walk unassisted down the hall and back. For a man who's made a living in the outdoors since he was sixteen, confinement to a bed was unacceptable and Howard got out in three days. Not long after, he was lifting 80-pound bags from the water. The 73-year old bayman is in perpetual motion. One year he entered an outboard hydroplane he built of mahogany and fiberglass in several races on a Connecticut reservoir. Oystering now keeps him too busy for more frequent racing, but years ago he beat more than 100 competitors to win the national championship for A-stock hydro-planes, and in 2005 he took first place at a regional meet in Standish, Maine. Pickerell says he achieves higher speeds by "remanufacturing" his engine and propellers.

Howard also is renowned among other baymen for the rugged workboats he builds at his shop in Water Mill. His stable, open garveys feature a blunt bow, progressive vee-bottom, and low free-board to make it easier to haul aboard shellfish. He says, "George Washington crossed the Delaware in a garvey. That's why he could stand up without tipping the boat. But it wasn't one of mine."

Pickerell has worked Long Island waters for sixty-five years. While still a youngster, he built his own clam boat, studied diesel engines, and later took a night course in aquaculture which helps him read bathymetric maps of Long Island waters. Over the years he's built some 550 boats, more than half of them garveys for clammers in Great South Bay when clams were abundant there. In Alaska a tough, 18-foot Pickerell garvey salvaged logs that broke away from logging rafts being floated to sawmills, earning $100 each for the man who lassoed them. He also builds down-east style boats from 24 to 32 feet. One served as a dive boat in Antigua, another tended telephone lines in Casco Bay, Maine. They've become popular too as "picnic" boats, admired for their salty resemblance to Maine lobster boats.

Lobster pot markers adorn a house on the harbor.

Howard brings us back to the days before Sag Harbor became a Hampton's attraction, when the Peconics were afloat more with workboats than luxury yachts. Next time you slurp a dozen local oysters, think of Howard Pickerell and other baymen who were here long before most of us, making a living on the water through hard work and ingenuity, and lending our village an authenticity that charms everyone who comes to visit.

❋ ❋ ❋

The Most Important Fish in the World

Before becoming a captain of industry, I worked during the summer as a humble "parkie" for the New York City Dept. of Parks picking up litter from the beach in the Rockaways. I also raked the shoreline, usually seaweed, but occasionally dead moss bunkers, properly known as menhaden, that washed up at high tide the night before. A little truck with fat tires would come along and we'd pitchfork the smelly fish into the truck's bin. The load went to a landfill but we didn't care where they went, we just wanted to be rid of them. At the time we wouldn't have believed that the smelly, unwanted fish would ever be called the most important catch in the world.

An article in the *New York Times* in 2016 was headlined "Not Just Another Stinky Fish." With a little digging, especially in an old issue of *Discovery Magazine*, we found that menhaden are oily, full of tiny bones and rich in fat. No one eats them but they can be ground up, dried and become a high-protein food for chickens, pigs, cattle, and domestic pets. Fishermen catch menhaden to use as bait in lobster traps or to lure striped bass. When still in the ocean, menhaden supply key sustenance for bass, mackerel, cod, swordfish, bluefish, and tuna. Perhaps most important, menhaden swim in schools of hundreds of thousands and act as giant filter feeders. They suck up huge amounts of phytoplankton which, containing nitrogen and phosphorous, cause algae growth and red and brown tides. Surprisingly, menhaden contributed to the demise of the whaling industry in Sag Harbor, but more on that later.

The Atlantic menhaden is a member of the herring family. An average adult is 9 to 12 inches long, weighs up to a pound, and yields half an ounce of oil. Because of all the benefits they produce, and the danger that their depletion would damage major ecosystems, state fisheries along the Atlantic Coast have been keeping track of the stock of menhaden in the sea. Which brings us to Omega Protein, a Houston company which is the country's largest harvester of menhaden and marketer of a wildly popular health supplement. The company's original parent, Zapata, was co-founded by former president George H. W. Bush in 1953.

Omega Protein became independent in 1998 after taking over several competitors. For years Omega Protein has flown spotter planes to locate enormous menhaden schools, sometimes as large as a football field and reaching 100-feet below the surface. The planes radio the locations of the schools to 170-foot long processing ships which then launch a couple of smaller boats. These deploy enormous purse seines that encircle the fish, as many as 50,000 at a time. The bigger vessel then pulls alongside and pumps the catch into its hold. The *New York Times* said last year that Omega Protein has harvested an annual catch of 188,000 metric tons to be rendered into heart-healthy omega-3 fatty acid fish oil, with the remnants going into fertilizers and animal feed.

In 2012, to protect the ocean stock of menhaden, the Atlantic States Marine Fisheries Commission, a consortium of 15 states from Maine to Florida, reduced the allowable harvest of menhaden by 20 percent. The reduction was changed to 10 percent in 2015 when regulators decided the fish was not being over-harvested. Sports fishermen, commercial interests, state lawmakers, and environmental groups constantly squabble over fishing quotas.

Richard Schiffman, a journalist who covers environmental issues, says that when commercial interests triumph over sound science, the result can be environmentally catastrophic. He says that's what happened to New England's groundfish industry, especially cod, which was declared a federal disaster in 2012. On the other hand, he quotes Joseph Gordon of the Pew Charitable Trusts who said that the commission's effort to develop a holistic strategy for managing menhaden is an exciting precedent since it values the fish "not just for what it provides when taken from the sea, but for what it provides when it is kept in the ocean."

Bunkers go far back in history. Algonquian Indians taught the pilgrims to plant menhaden with corn seeds to produce a better crop, especially from depleted soil. In fact, the name "menhaden" stems from an Algonquin word meaning "to enrich." After the Civil War, America's growing machine industry found menhaden oil a cheaper alternative to whale oil, contributing to the demise of the whaling industry and to Sag Harbor's local economy. Many Sag Harbor whalemen gladly gave up years-long voyages on dangerous seas to pursue more accessible, less dangerous bunkers in nearby waters. Sag Harbor, Greenport, Shelter Island, and Amagansett, especially east along the Napeague stretch, became heavily involved in netting and processing menhaden, obviously not just another stinky fish.

Why Our Barber Climbed Kilimanjaro

C hoppin' Charlie's Barber Shop, across from the post office, has become a popular member of the Sag Harbor business community. Besides good grooming for the dudes in the village, the biggest reason for its popularity is its attractive owner, April Jakubauskas. At first glance, April appears to be no more or less than a successful entrepreneur with a deft touch with the scissors. But she is much more than that, having survived a deadly fight with blood cancer, rugged treatment including stem cells from a donor in Germany, and the celebration of her recovery with a climb to the top of a 20,000-ft mountain.

April says her medical ordeal completely changed the way she looks at the world and sees her own life. She says she no longer feels the need for anything more than she has, to acquire more "things." She adds, "In a strange way I'm actually thankful for my struggle because without it, I wouldn't have discovered my strength."

April's saga began in October 2012 when she was diagnosed with multiple myeloma (MM), a cancer of the plasma cells that produce antibodies we need to keep us healthy. The disease is generally considered incurable. For months she had suffered pain in her ribs along with extreme fatigue and nasty bouts with shingles and sciatica. Visits with several doctors provided little relief or insight to the problem.

Finally a bone marrow test revealed the dangerous disease. A friend referred her to Dr Alexander Lesokhin at Sloan Kettering Memorial Hospital in Manhattan who labelled her affliction as Stage 3 multiple myeloma with secondary plasma-cell leukemia. Ironically the leukemia element was considered a positive finding because it meant the disease could be treated with stem cell protocols. She was admitted to Sloan Kettering on October 21st for induction chemotherapy and after four days began heavy chemo twice a week.

At that point April found it difficult and painful even to walk, but she was told she must build herself up for a transplant of her own stem cells. She flew to an aunt's house in California and for weeks embarked on a regimen of exercise and nutrition. This first transplant took place in March of 2013. But Sloan Kettering doctors warned her that the disease would come back unless she received a second stem cell transplant from a donor. They also knew that Germany maintains a register of the DNA of its citizens, and they asked the medical community there if anyone on the list was a match for April's genes.

Fortunately a young woman named Katrin Kormann who matched nine of ten critical genes was identified and she agreed to become the donor. It took four hours for a hospital in Germany to harvest Katrin's blood cells which then were flown to Sloan Kettering. Immediately they were infused into April. A planned course of severe chemo already had reduced April's immune system so that the donor's stem cells would be accepted.

From that crucial point April fought back, often nauseous but forcing herself to take nutrition. After 31 days at Sloan, she went to Hope Lodge, a hotel-like facility in Manhattan supported by the American

Cancer Society. She continued to return to Sloan for blood transfusions to bolster her red cells. It was three months before she was somewhat better, and in 2014 she felt strong enough to work part-time at her barber shop. During her long absence for treatment, her father, a retired aeronautical engineer, and her brother, went to barbering school to learn the craft and keep the business going. Two years ago, to the delight of her customers, she finally returned full-time to Choppin' Charlie's. The new stem cells changed her blood type and so altered her blood system that she had to repeat all her childhood vaccinations.

At a fund-raiser in Manhattan in May 2016 for the Multiple Myeloma Research Foundation (MMRF), April learned that Takeda Pharmaceutical Company Ltd., a source of drugs to treat multiple myeloma, was sponsoring a climb of Mt. Kilimanjaro in Tanzania to raise awareness of the disease and publicize MMRF's work. At 19,341-feet Kilimanjaro is the highest peak in Africa and fourth highest in the world. Though not a technical climb, its biggest challenge is due to altitude. And because the terrain is mostly volcanic ash, climbers tend to slip back from each step they take.

Once again, a determined April began body-building to prepare for the expedition. This past February, in a group of sixteen, including a doctor, several care givers and five other patients, April reached the summit in seven days. On the wall of the barber shop is a photo of her at the top of Kilimanjaro dressed in bulky, cold weather clothing, thoroughly exhausted, but proud of what she had accomplished after her long battle with cancer.

From Tanzania, April flew to Cologne where she met Katrin, her stem cell donor. She said at first they just stood and smiled at each other, tears coming to her eyes for what the German girl had done for her. They hugged and spent the day exchanging personal stories, April bragging a little bit about climbing Kilimanjaro.

6

Writers, Artists, and Personalities

John Steinbeck's Sag Harbor

"Out here I get the old sense of peace and whole-ness…and it seems to be getting into my work. I ap-proach the table every morning with a sense of joy."
—from a note to his publisher in 1956.

"I grow into this countryside with a lichen grip."
—in a letter to friend and fellow novelist John O'Hara in 1958.

Steinbeck won the 1940 Pulitzer Prize for *The Grapes of Wrath*, and in 1962 was awarded the Nobel Prize for Literature for his novels, short stories and sketches. In September 1953 he rented a waterfront cottage in Sag Harbor, and in 1955 bought a small house in an oak grove on Sag Harbor Cove. He wrote a friend, "I really love it out here. Am going to winterize this little house so I can come up when it is cold. I haven't felt so good in years." And later, "We love our little place on Long Island."

In the spring 1992 issue of the *Long Island Historical Journal* Frances Kestler quoted a Steinbeck letter about autumn in Sag Harbor, "Almost my favorite season. For some reason it brings a kind of happy energy back to me. The birds are flocking and flying. The geese go over at night very high. And the air has muscle." While working on a modern version of Thomas Malory's *Morte d'Arthur* in January 1957 he wrote his editor Elizabeth Otis that "the bay is nearly frozen over with just a few patches of open water…. Charlie [his dog] is having a wonderful time trying to walk on the ice." Steinbeck's tiny writing hideaway, that he called Joyous Garde after Launcelot's castle, stood away from the house, closer to the cove. A year later he told Otis about the "solace I get from the new boat (in Sag Harbor). I can move out and anchor and have a little table and a yellow pad and pencil. Nothing can intervene. Isn't that wonderful?"

Steinbeck called his little writing studio "Joyous Garde."

Steinbeck helped start the Old Whalers Festival (now Harborfest) in the early sixties and was made its honorary chairman. He happily joined in the fun, writing official words of welcome,

> The fact that I have been made Honorary Chairman of the Old Whaler's Festival is a clear indication of the explosive but cautious thinking of the descendants of the Old Whalers. If all goes well we share the happiness, but if the village blows up, I get the blame. I don't know how I got here. I'm only a sixth class citizen. It takes six generations for first class...."

In their delightful collection of Sag Harbor stories, Maryann Calendrille and Kathryn Szoka of Canio's Books included Steinbeck's essay "My War With the Ospreys" that reflected his love of the village.

> Two and a half years ago I bought a little place near Sag Harbor... a wonderful village inhabited by people who have been here for a long time.... The place I bought is not one of the great old houses but a beautiful little point of land on the inland waters, a place called Bluff Point, with its own little bay.... My own boat, the *Lillymaid*... is a utility craft twenty feet long, a clinker-built Jersey sea skiff.... Many of these specifications could also describe my wife. She is not clinker-built however.... I came from a small town on the West Coast... and I find that what applies in my home country is equally acceptable in Sag Harbor. If you pay your bills, trade locally as much as possible, mind your own business and act reasonably pleasant, pretty soon they forget that you are an outsider."

In *The True Adventures of John Steinbeck, Writer*, biographer Jackson J. Benson described Steinbeck's simple daily habits, "...sometimes later in the day after work he'd stop by and ask Bob Barry out for a beer at Sal and Joe's or the Black Buoy."

John was afflicted with back and heart problems in 1967 and was treated in New York City, but yearned to come back to Sag Harbor.

> ...to go out to my little house on the point, to sharpen fifty pencils and put out a yellow pad. Early in the morning to hear what the birds are saying and to pass the time of day with Angel [Charley's successor] and then to hunch up my chair to my writing board and to set down with words — Once upon a time....

Steinbeck's recurring heart problems worsened in November 1968 and he again was taken to a hospital in New York City, leaving his beloved Sag Harbor for the last time. He died on December 20th.

Einstein Wasn't Much of a Sailor

In September 1939 Hitler invaded Poland, starting World War II and inflicting years of suffering on the world. Only a couple of months earlier, Albert Einstein vacationed for the summer in a rented cottage on Nassau Point, across Little Peconic Bay from Noyac, not knowing he would play a reluctant part in ending the war. In July two refugee physicists from Hungary, Leo Szilard, then at Columbia University, and Eugene Wigner of Princeton, drove out to the North Fork to talk to Einstein. They had information that German scientists had smashed the atom and were working to develop a nuclear weapon. They feared that, if successful, it could well enable Hitler to dominate the free world. They wanted Einstein's help in convincing the Roosevelt administration to take action against the looming danger. Einstein met the two physicists and though concerned about the morality of creating such a doomsday device, he wrote a letter that eventually reached Roosevelt. It helped persuade him to order the secret American effort, called the Manhattan Project, to build an atomic bomb.

One of Einstein's pleasures that summer was sailing a 14-foot catboat called *Tinef* which means Junk in Yiddish, and according to Dr. Marilyn Weigold of Pace University, writing in the Summer 2000 issue of *Long Island Forum*, local boys came to Einstein's aid when he capsized the little boat in a strong breeze. One of the boys, Robert Fisher, gave Einstein boating advice but said that the 60-year old scientist never got the hang of sailing. The Nobel Laureate more enjoyed playing Bach on his violin, joined by David Rothman who ran the local department store. They discovered their mutual love of music when Rothman sold Einstein a pair of sandals. Walter Isaacson gives a similar account in his fine biography of Einstein.

Isaacson quotes Szilard on their search for the scientist, "We knew that Einstein was somewhere on Long Island, but we didn't know precisely where." Szilard called Einstein's Princeton office and was told he was renting the house of a Dr. Moore in the village of Peconic. After a number of misdirections they finally found him on Old Cove Road. Then, "sitting at a bare wooden table on the screen porch of the sparsely furnished cottage, Szilard reviewed the process of how an explosive chain reaction could be produced in uranium."

The three scientists agreed that a letter to the State Department signed by the famous Einstein might get proper attention. Fortunately Szilard later met Alexander Sachs, an economist at Lehman Brothers and a friend of Roosevelt, who offered to hand-deliver the letter to the president. But the letter needed revision and Szilard, this time accompanied by another refugee physicist, Edward Teller, drove out again to Peconic in Teller's 1935 Plymouth.

"Einstein dictated a revised letter in German," Szilard recalled, "which Teller took down, and I used this German text as a guide in preparing drafts of a letter to the President." It took months for Sachs to get in to see the President, and to the dismay of the Hungarian scientists who were extremely worried about Germany's progress towards the bomb, it wasn't until two years later, on December 6, 1941 that the United States finally launched the Manhattan Project. The resulting atomic bomb is credited by many historians as the deciding factor in ending the war with Japan.

According to Isaacson, Einstein was not asked to join the Manhattan Project or was even told about it, though he suspected the work had started when his physicist friends departed to obscure towns around the country. A few people in government, including FBI Director J. Edgar Hoover, thought Einstein a security risk because of pacifist and political groups he had supported in his past. Yet Vannevar Bush, director of the office supervising the Manhattan Project, asked for Einstein's help on a problem involving the separation of isotopes, and later in the war Einstein assisted the Navy in analyzing ordnance capabilities. The bushy-haired scientist joked "I am in the Navy but not required to get a Navy haircut."

When he heard that the atomic bomb had been dropped on Hiroshima with a huge loss of life, Einstein blurted out, "Oh, my God." He regretted his participation in development of nuclear weapons and began a political mission, says Isaacson, "that would dominate the remaining decade of Einstein's life" to create a world authority that could peacefully resolve disputes between nations.

The *Long Island Forum* article said that despite his sailing misadventures, Einstein considered his two summers on Little Peconic Bay the most enjoyable days of his life.

Writers and Artists Love It Here

As a scribbler myself, I have the feeling that people all over Sag Harbor are sitting at home in their little nooks scribbling away on a novel, a memoir, an article, an irate letter, whatever has unleashed their creative juices. Everyone I meet seems to be writing something. Sag Harbor has welcomed writers and artists since at least 1807. On February 9th that year the Literary Society of Sag Harbor was organized to "consist of Disputation, composition, Declamation, and examination upon Geography, Astronomy, and such other exercises as a majority shall appoint." According to The *History of the Town of Southampton* by James Truslow Adams, the duties of the treasurer of the society included furnishing "stationary, fuel, candles, &c" and was also to be a "Critic" whose duty was "to criticize upon all compositions and declamations." (Ah, a rare opportunity to put down other writers.) A system of fines was established for "gambling or intoxication outside of meetings, and no meeting should ever be held in a tavern" (an unexpected rule since writers have always had high regard for taverns).

Helen Harrison and Constance Demme depict literary and artistic life on the East End in their joyful book *Hamptons Bohemia: Two Centuries of Artists and Writers on the Beach*. They acknowledge the Sag Harbor Literary Society and say that fame really arrived later with the success of James Fenimore Cooper and Walt Whitman. Cooper came in 1819 and invested in a whaling venture. While staying at Duke Fordham's tavern on Main Street (society members must have been shocked) he wrote his first novel, *Precaution*, followed by *The Spy* and *The Pioneers* which launched his famous Leatherstocking Tales. Around the same time, Hubbard Latham Fordham began painting portraits of the local gentry. A distant cousin, Orlando Hand Bears, became even more successful as a portraitist and landscape artist. Before them, Anna Frances Sleight turned out water colors of the Sag scene as far back as 1803.

In the late 1800s William Merritt Chase established the Shinnecock School where he painted his renowned landscape and figure studies and attracted young artists including Annie Burnham Cooper from the prominent Sag Harbor family. In the early 1900s Childe Hassam of East Hampton and James Britton of Sag Harbor were inspired by East End scenes. Writers too found the Hamptons a source of pleasure and inspiration. In the 1920s leading New York City newspapermen Ring Lardner, Grantland Rice, and Irwin S. Cobb lived near each other in rented beach cottages.

According to *Hamptons Bohemia*, Sag Harbor's "most unorthodox art colonist" of the 1950s was Val Telberg, a photomontagist and film maker. He bought a house on Bay Street in 1956 and created haunting images of Trout Pond in Noyac. After World War II a number of literary figures ventured out to the South Fork, at least part time, and bought or rented homes in Sag Harbor and other East End communities. Over the years there were such luminaries as Kurt Vonnegut, Joseph Heller, James Salter, E. L. Doctorow, James Jones, John Knowles, Peter Matthiessen, Truman Capote, John Irving, Wilfrid

Canio's, Sag Harbor's iconic bookstore on Main Street.

Sheed, and Edward Albee. A photo of a smiling Doctorow swimming with his dog appears in the book.

The Eastville Artists, a colony of painters from Sag Harbor Hills, Azurest, and Ninevah, began exhibiting in the 1970s. Mostly African-American, the group included Nanette Carter, Alvin Loving, Frank Wimberley, and Robert Freeman. Guild Hall and the Parrish Art Museum supported local artists with exhibitions and competitions.

The roster of East End artists and writers is endless. There were Willem de Kooning, Larry Rivers, and Jackson Pollock whose paintings command millions of dollars years after their deaths. A *New York Times* article in 1998 recounted the names of famous East End writers and artists, then went on to talk about a new wave coming to the Hamptons, "They are young and old, eccentric and straight-laced. They paint canvases in oil, sculpture stone and metal, mix watercolors

195

and take photographs. They write novels, novellas, poetry, travel-ogues, science fiction, non-fiction and articles for major newspapers and literary reviews."

So my first impression is surely correct. If you listen closely you can probably hear writers and artists all over Sag Harbor and neighboring villages endlessly tapping out immortal words and daubing genius paint on canvas. And we are all the richer for it.

❋ ❋ ❋

James Fenimore Cooper: Author, Whaler, Hell Raiser

If you paid attention in school, you know that James Fenimore Cooper, born in 1789, was the world-famous author of Early American novels. If you're up on local lore, you probably know that he financed a couple of whaling expeditions out of Sag Harbor. But did you know that Cooper was thrown out of Yale in his third year for blowing up the door of another student, and while still a young man he was embroiled in numerous law suits over money he owed? In later years he stirred things up in Europe and fought bitter libel battles with newspaper editors.

When Cooper came out on the short end of a fracas with fel-low Yalie, John Boyle, he mixed gunpowder in the college lab and poured it into the keyhole of Boyle's dormitory door. The explosion naturally frightened Boyle and did considerable damage to the door. All of this and more is detailed in *James Fenimore Cooper The Early Years*, a biography by Professor Wayne Franklin of the University of Connecticut.

Though Cooper was taunted by critics — one called his works "monumental in their cumulative dullness" — he holds a prominent place in literary history. Says Professor Franklin, Cooper was the first to write major types of American fiction — Westerns, Sea Tales, Revolutionary War romances — all of which influenced future American writers. *Encyclopedia Brittanica* calls him the first major novelist of the United States. He is best known for his wilderness books, the Leatherstocking Tales, which included *The Last of the Mohicans*, *The Deerslayer,* and *The Pathfinder*, and introduced famous literary figures Natty Bumppo, Hawkeye, and Uncas. Cooper's novels reflected the emerging character of the infant republic, and were presciently sensitive to the environment and the plight of Native Americans.

Cooper went to sea in 1806 at the age of 17 as a merchant seaman, and a couple of years later became a midshipman in the U.S. Navy. He came from a distinguished family, his father a Federalist Congressman who founded Cooperstown in Upstate New York. When his father died, James inherited sizable land holdings along with many debts. He borrowed money from another Yale man and when he later questioned the usurious rates of the loan, a legal dispute dragged on in the courts for years.

In 1811 Cooper married Susan Augusta DeLancey from Mamaroneck who had relatives among the established Dering, Nicoll, and Sylvester families of Sag Harbor and Shelter Island. In visits to the East End Cooper became friends with Charles T. Dering whose mother was a Sylvester, a prosperous clan from Shelter Island. Charles's uncle was Henry P. Dering, a leading citizen of Sag Harbor and its first custom collector.

Cooper thought whaling could be a way out of his tight circumstances and he partnered with Charles Dering to buy *Union*, a 260-ton, 92-ft vessel. Outfitting *Union* for its first whaling voyage cost $5,000, nearly $100,000 in today's money, forcing Cooper to sell some of the land he inherited. The first whale hunt off Brazil and Patagonia was successful and after paying the captain and crew, Cooper realized around $10,000. He spent a large chunk of it to outfit *Union* for a second voyage and was soon borrowing again, using the ship as collateral.

In 1820 Cooper published his first novel *Precaution*, but his big break came in 1823 when the novel *Pioneers* launched the popular Leatherstocking series. His financial condition improved considerably and in 1826 Cooper took his family to Paris where he had many admirers, remaining there for seven years. During that time he spoke out against right-wing movements in Europe. At the same time he was criticized back in the U.S. by newspapers allied with the Whigs, a forerunner of the Republican Party. The newspapers were sympathetic to French rightists and in opposition to President Andrew Jackson's espousal of an egalitarian society. The battles intensified when Cooper returned home and published *A Letter to His Countrymen* which criticized American culture. Suits and countersuits raged. Cooper won most of the conflicts but felt his reputation had been sullied, making him more private and protective of his personal papers which only became fully available in the early 1990s.

When we studied early American fiction, it was easy to mistake Cooper, with his posh-sounding name, as a fusty, wealthy patrician with distinguished family connections. But in his early years he had to scramble just to support his wife and family, and between his college days at Yale and the end of his life he never shied away from a fight.

Wilfrid Sheed Was Our Gift to Baseball

I've been angry at baseball ever since the Dodgers departed Brooklyn and left me with the soul-crushing Mets, so much so that I don't go to games anymore. At least I didn't until I stumbled across *Baseball and Lesser Sports* by the late Harborite Wilfrid

Sheed. Published in 1991, it's a collection of Sheed's sports articles that appeared in a long list of publications. His insights and surprising turns-of-phrase have inspired me to watch baseball again, at least at Mashashimuet Park where the college boys are gamboling around the basepaths.

Before his death in January 2011, Sheed whimsically suggested an inscription for his headstone,

> He wrote some good sentences.

Answering the critics who complained about the slowness of the game, British-born Sheed described his initial impression of baseball.

> That was how it looked at first — boys milling around dusty lots jabbering and hitching at their pants. But as I kept craning from train windows and car windows in my first days in America, I noticed something promising; that nothing ever seemed to be happening at that particular moment — the same basic principle as cricket.... Baseball was not as busy as it seemed but lived, like the mother game, on pregnant pauses.

Responding to snobs who looked down on sports, Sheed wrote, "Baseball and other sports are alternatives to life, stories we tell ourselves to take our minds off life but also to add something to it, as art itself does." He brought freshness to normally cliché-ridden sportswriting. About life in the minor leagues, "The paint peels in the locker room and the shower stalls would wring a complaint from a guerilla leader or a nineteenth century English schoolboy." Or about retired ball players, "A guy who's played one game in the pros is like a former state senator, a big man in most neighborhoods, and in any saloon, as long as he lives."

He covered other sports equally well, such as this on pro football's offensive linemen:

Every play in the book requires of them a different nuance of blocking — whether to make a hole or only appear to, whether to brush block or steamroller or even occasionally to let a man through while appearing not to (the primeval "mousetrap" play) — and these plays are often changed at the line of scrimmage, while our man is staring at an enraged, hyperactive gorilla a few feet away and trying to decipher the quarterback's signals over the howl of the crowd.

Wilfrid Sheed loved Sag Harbor, coming here full-time in 1972. "In those days, before the crowds moved in, I liked Sag Harbor. Nobody knew or cared what I did for a living. It was like New York City east. You heard Brooklyn accents and there were almost as many saloons." He recalled beating Sag Harbor artist Cappy Amundsen in a game of pool at the Black Buoy Bar, one of the few people who ever did. His comic novel, *The Boys of Winter*, involves a softball league of writers and artists in a village in the Hamptons that could only be Sag Harbor.

His parents, Francis Joseph Sheed and Maisie Ward, were publishers in London, and later in the States after they emigrated to escape German bombings. Once the war ended, and after earning degrees from Oxford, Sheed wrote for the *New York Times Book Review,* the *New Yorker* and other prominent magazines. He was prolific, producing nine novels and seven books of non-fiction. His final work, *The House That George Built: With a Little Help From Irving, Cole and a Crew of About Fifty,* came out in 2007, a critically acclaimed best seller about the musical era he loved.

A baseball purist, Sheed criticized changes to the game. "The dh (designated hitter) rule is a prime example of how to give superficial pleasure to superficial fans. It means you never have to watch a lemon at the bat, with all his mad hopes and sorrows, and life becomes one unbroken parade of experts." He remembered his childhood years after arriving in the States.

I became perhaps the outstanding solitary baseball player of my generation, whaling fungoes down the long, narrow garden and plodding after them, chattering to myself and whaling them back again…. When that paled, I would chalk a strike zone on the garage door and lob a tennis ball at it. Already I had the style, though God knows where it came from: the mock aggression and inscrutable loneliness. Gary Cooper high on a hill, twitching his cap, shaking off the sign: nodding, rearing, firing. Clunk, against the old garage door.

See you at Mashashimuet Park. Play ball!

✳ ✻ ✳

Irving Berlin Brought Showbiz to Camp Upton

July 4th is a perfect time to remember Irving Berlin, his ties with Long Island, and what he meant to the nation. He wrote the music and lyrics of our favorite songs, including "God Bless America," which many people think should be our national anthem. It was first sung by Kate Smith on her radio show in 1938. Berlin explained years later that the song's title came from his mother who often whispered the words as a prayer of thanks for living in the United States. The renowned George Gershwin, another refugee from Russia, called him "the greatest songwriter that ever lived."

Berlin's father, a cantor in a synagogue, fled oppression in Russia and brought his wife and eight children here in 1893 when Irving was five years old. Life wasn't easy. They were crammed into a tenement on Cherry Street in the lower east side of New York City and Irving scrambled for menial jobs to make a few pennies to drop into his mother's apron. He sold newspapers, sang in saloons, taught himself to play the piano, and became a singing waiter at a cafe in Chinatown.

His first song "Marie From Sunny Italy" earned him 37 cents. Then in 1911, at age 30, Berlin wrote "Alexander's Ragtime Band" which became a giant hit, sparked a national dance craze, and launched his reputation.

Berlin went on to create such iconic tunes as "Easter Parade," "White Christmas," "There's No Business Like Show Business," "Always," "Blue Skies," "What'll I Do," "A Pretty Girl Is Like a Melody," and "I've Got My Love to Keep Me Warm." People of a certain age can still hum the music and even remember some of the lyrics. He wrote some 1,500 songs, many introduced in his 18 films and 19 Broadway musicals, including *Annie Get Your Gun* and *Call Me Madam*. He composed on Long Island during both World Wars, initially stationed with the Army at Camp Upton in World War I where he wrote the musical *Yip! Yip! Yaphank*, and again during World War II when he wrote *This Is the Army*. Both shows went from Camp Upton to successful runs on Broadway.

Berlin frequently visited his daughter Mary Ellin Barrett who owned a second home in Water Mill. After his death the U.S. Postal Service released a commemorative stamp at a ceremony in Times Square. An article in the *Long Island Forum*, Spring 2003 issue, said that his daughter asked for a second ceremony at the Water Mill post office which was held in September 2002. She recounted that her father was deeply grateful to the United States for giving him the chance to rise from poverty and he assigned his millions of dollars of royalties from "God Bless America" to the Girl and Boy Scouts. He also rejected advice to use tax shelters saying "I want to pay taxes, I love this country."

Berlin's first wife died of typhus only six months after their wedding. He later married Ellin Mackay, a young socialite whose father objected to the union, but they eloped and embarked on a marriage of 63 years and four children. Irving died in 1989 at the age of 101. Walter Cronkite said Berlin, "helped write the story of this country, capturing the best of who we are and the dreams that shape our lives."

Yaphank, the little hamlet near Camp Upton used in the name of the World War I show, was originally known as Millville, but when the residents applied for a post office, they were told that the name already existed in New York state. So they chose Yaphank, adapted from a native American place name, figuring there couldn't be another town with that designation. Troops on pass from Camp Upton usually sought fun and games in the larger town of Patchogue.

Camp Upton, named for a Civil War general, had a checkered history in the service of the country. At the end of World War I, it was deactivated as an Army training post and the buildings sold or dismantled, some of them reappearing as homes for Long Islanders. During the Great Depression, the site housed units of the Civilian Conservation Corps. World War II brought it back again as a military hospital and rehabilitation center. Berlin volunteered to return to Upton and raise money for the Army Emergency Relief Fund. That's where he staged *This Is the Army* appearing in the production himself singing "Oh, How I Hate to Get Up in the Morning."

In 1947, Upton was turned over to the Atomic Energy Commission and renamed Brookhaven National Laboratory, mandated to research peaceful uses of the atom. Berlin would have written a song about it; only the master music man could have rhymed something with Brookhaven.

※ ✺ ※

Doctoring by Horse and Stanley Steamer

Born in Amagansett in 1848, a graduate of Bellevue Hospital Medical School, Dr. Edgar B. Mulford lived in Bridgehampton and cared for patients from Quogue to Montauk Point. Medical science in the late 1800s and early 1900s when Mulford practiced had little resemblance to what we know today. It took until 1901, for example, to discover the existence of different blood types. In 1906 it was agreed that lack of vitamins might cause scurvy and rickets. Only during those early years did the theory of germs and the use of anesthesia in surgery enter medical practice. A century ago, before the evening news became jammed with TV ads touting treatments for cancer, depression, COPD, and a dozen other ailments, newspaper ads promised that Ready Relief medicine was good for "sore throat, bronchitis, tonsillitis, and all inflammations." Ayer's Sarsaparilla "purified the blood and made the weak strong." Coe's Lotion cured eczema, and best of all, Hall's Wine was "the Supreme Tonic Restorative." Well, at least that hasn't changed.

Edgar Mulford practiced medicine on the East End for more than 40 years. He held visiting hours on Sunday and in the morning a large number of horse-drawn rigs of all types would be lined up outside his house. In an old issue of the *Long Island Forum*, Howard Hendrickson describes a visit to the front room of Dr. Mulford's large home in Bridgehampton. "Opening off this office was a roomy closet that showed shelves holding…hundreds of bottles of all shapes and sizes and filled to varying degrees with pills and liquids of all colors. Office fee was fifty cents."

Before automobiles and decent roads, country doctors depended on road horses. A busy practice was measured in the number of road horses kept. Mulford loved horses and a couple of miles from his home he kept some twenty mares, foals, colts, and a stallion. When the doctor returned home to refill a medicine bag, or just to get warm and have something to eat, he hooked up a fresh horse to continue his calls. One account says that on a winter day Mulford used three teams of horses in covering sixty miles. There were no drugstore prescriptions, the doctor probably carried vials of morphine, atropine, strychnine, and digitalis. When Mulford entered a home where a man or woman was living alone, he might find the patient in bed and the fire out. After treating the patient, he would build a fire, cook some food, feed the patient, leave medicine, and tell a neighbor how to care for the lone invalid.

The *Forum* article tells an amazing story of Dr. Mulford returning from a call on a winter afternoon when his horse Dolly fell from fatigue. The doctor covered the animal with a blanket and his own lap robe and lay down back-to-back with the horse. After a while Dolly felt better, got to her feet, or hooves, and they continued on their way home. Mulford told friends, "Dolly was tired and I was tired too." When he drove his buggy in winter over frozen, rutted roads, the doctor dressed in heavy wool underwear and woolen suits, and cloth arctics pulled up over his shoes almost to his knees. An ulster coat also of heavy wool protected him from his ankles up to a heavy collar that could be pulled up to the head. A hat with ear flaps might be added.

In later years, Hendrickson remembers Dr. Mulford being driven about by his son in a Stanley Steamer. "In February of 1926, at the age of 78, Dr. Mulford, bag in hand, wading through the snow to a patient, suffered a heart attack and passed away," a great loss to the East End and to the medical profession.

✳ ✳ ✳

Harbor Pharmacist Became an Authority on Algonquin Language

When he was five years old, William Wallace Tooker became fascinated with the history and language of the Native Americans on eastern Long Island. He had found an Algonquin flint near Conkling's Point and subsequently roamed all over Sag Harbor and the surrounding countryside, discovering broken pottery, arrowheads, and working tools. His findings are now part of the Smithsonian's National Museum of the American Indian. Born in Sag Harbor in 1848 at the family home on Hampton Street, he was the grandson of famous portrait painter Hubbard Fordham and a great grandson of David Frothingham, editor of Long Island's first newspaper.

Tooker hoped to enter Yale University, but financial pressure forced him to go to work at age 18 as an apprentice at a Sag Harbor pharmacy. That didn't stop him from collecting more than 15,000 artifacts of early Indian life. The list is extensive — axes, adzes, hoes, chisels, fleshers and skinning knives, gougers, hammers, sinkers, sharpening and grinding stones, choppers, pipes, ornaments, spear points, mortars and about a thousand "perfect" arrowheads. He restored a pottery vessel from a grave near Otter Pond and discovered a large number of artifacts from a shell heap nearby. Tooker befriended the last of the old Algonquin families, the Pharaohs and Fowlers of Montauk, and the Bunns, Cuffees, and Kellises of Shinnecock, absorbing everything they could teach him. His research and diggings revealed remains of Indian wigwams in the area along today's Bay Street, and extensive crafting of wampum that was often traded with Dutch visitors.

Tooker was one of five children of William Henry Tooker, a Sag Harbor merchant whose family came from England to Massachusetts in the 17th century. His mother Virginia Victoria Ford was a descendent of Reverend Robert Fordham, a 17th century minister in Southampton. While working as a pharmacist in Sag Harbor, Tooker became "the foremost student of Coastal Algonquin life, and he exerted an important influence on the development of the field." So wrote Lois Beachy Underhill in the spring 1999 edition of the *Long Island Historical Journal*.

Most of Tooker's papers are now in Cornell University Library's Division of Rare and Manuscript Collections. The library's website notes that Tooker published 12 books, some 50 pamphlets and over 100 articles between 1888 and 1911, and as late as the 1960s, his studies were the standard for publishers of Long Island history. The New York Public Library, the Library of Congress and our own John Jermain Library possess collections of his writing. Publisher Francis P. Harper bought out ten of Tooker's major papers in a limited edition entitled *The Algonquin Series* that is still consulted by specialists in Indian history.

Tooker regularly was asked to present papers before scholarly organizations such as the American Association for the Advancement of Science. Though not formerly trained in linguistics or ethnology, he wrote articles for major scholarly journals including *American Anthropologist* and *The Archeologist*. In 1887, the editor of the *Brooklyn Eagle Almanac* asked him to compile a list of Long Island Indian place names which became a regular feature of the publication. According to the Cornell Library, Tooker's work was exacting. He once wrote a 75-page essay on the origin of the name Manhattan, explaining that it translated into Hilly Island, a combination of the Delaware Indian term for island, mannah, with the northern Algonquin suffix for hills, atin.

Tooker was childhood friends with Lilla Byram Cartwright, daughter of Captain Thomas Cartwright of Shelter Island and Mary Winters of Sag Harbor. Tooker and Lilla married in 1872 and moved into a house on Hampton Street originally built by whaleship owner, Charles Thomas Dering. They were childless and devoted themselves to one another for 37 years. Tooker acquired the pharmacy in 1875 and the business supported them for 22 years until poor health brought on his retirement in 1897.

Tooker researched early records of the Dutch and English colonists and recorded any Indian place names he found. Worsening health and money problems dogged his declining years and he was forced to sell his Indian artifact collection to the Brooklyn Museum in 1901. Anxious to help him work on his book *Indian Place Names on Long Island*, Mrs. Russell Sage, Sag Harbor's great benefactor, established a trust fund for his support. Nursed by his wife and aided by secretaries retained by Mrs. Sage, he was able to complete the book and see it printed in 1911. Cornell says it is a classic study of its type and a lasting memorial to Tooker's scholarship.

Cappy, a Memorable Harbor Character

The jacket photo on the front of Terry Wallace's book *Cappy, the Life and Art of C. Hjalmar Amundsen*, is of a healthy, rugged-looking man in the prime of life. On the back of the book jacket is a smaller photo of an old man, with a scraggly beard and a shrunken, boney face. The two photos are of the same man, Cappy Amundsen, a memorable member of the Sag Harbor community for over 50 years, from the late 1940s to his death in 2001. He became a famous painter of marine scenes and, though he died nearly 20 years ago, his distinctive art is still displayed in homes and businesses all over the village.

The two photos reflect not only the passage of time, but also the hard knocks that often come with the erratic lives of many artists. At one point in a span of a few years, Cappy sold more than 500 paintings and was in demand for calendars and magazine covers, during a later period he exchanged his art for a meal or a drink at Sag Harbor bars and restaurants. But through good times and bad, Cappy remained a beloved friend to all who knew him, including John Steinbeck, John Ward, Paul Babcock, Kurt Vonnegut, Bobby Van, and Wilfrid Sheed. Tony Pintauro was a close pal, and in Cappy's fading years helped care for him.

Born June 9, 1911 in Williamsport, Pennsylvania, his christened name Caspar led eventually to the nickname Cappy. His father was a successful artist and illustrator who later moved his family to New York City. Cappy attended Blair Academy where he was a good athlete in many sports. He first saw Sag Harbor when his father brought him out to fish on the East End. In his early years, during the depression, Cappy lived much of the time in Greenwich Village while studying art at the University of the State of New York under a WPA program. He helped start the annual Washington Square Outdoor Art Show which grew into an important event.

Cappy Amundsen during better days.

From 1934 to 1942 Cappy worked in Provincetown and Gloucester, Massachusetts as a commercial fisherman, lobsterman and fishing guide, jobs that brought him close familiarity with work-boats and harbor scenes. He continued painting and taking classes, and began to introduce into his art a distinctive treatment of light and shadow. Along with many artists at that time, he also joined the Industrial Workers of the World, known as the Wobblies, a socialist workers union. In 1936, the *New York Herald Tribune* featured Cappy in its coverage of the Washington Square Art Show. "The seascapes of Hjalmar Amundsen... have almost become a tradition in the show. His rich tones in harbor scenes and portraits of dock hands and sea-faring folk evidence a strong conviction that the Scandinavian artist once sailed the seas himself." Actually Cappy never lived in Norway but felt ties through his grandparents.

Cappy signed his paintings with many aliases, possibly because at one time he turned out so much art that he was afraid he would glut the market. During World War II, rated 4F by his draft board, Cappy published a portfolio of Naval ships which proved quite popular. In the late 1940s he produced a series of large seascapes which added hugely to his reputation and popularity. In 1946, he married Nancy Williams Denison and moved to Sag Harbor. He and Nancy competed in their Snipe Class racing sailboat *Fancy Nancy* and later in outboard races. In May 1948 Nancy gave birth to a daughter.

Cappy entered into community life in the village donating his art to local charities such as the LVIS and helping form a Sea Scout Troop. He contributed sketches to the *Sag Harbor Express* and for a couple of years wrote a column called "Whales' Tales and Sag Harbor Scuttlebutt." Between 1950 and 1953 he sold 547 canvasses, but a trend to abstract impressionism loomed in the art world and between 1954 and 1956 he sold only 50 paintings.

Author Wallace who owns an art gallery in East Hampton and shows a number of Cappy's paintings, says that Sag Harbor was full of drinkers when Cappy came here and it was impossible for him to stay sober. Cappy also preferred fishing and sailing to working and grew lax in supporting his family. Sometime after 1956 Nancy asked for a divorce and at the same time his favorite art dealer died. He began spending more hours in the Black Buoy and the original Baron's Cove. (Wilfrid Sheed bragged that he was the only one to beat Cappy in a game of pool.) After Nancy left him, he drank more and in the 1970s began lapsing in health. As his home fell into disrepair, Paul Babcock said, "He started tearing up floorboards and carving whale forms out of them to sell."

Near the end, Cappy had to hitch rides around town. Eventually he was admitted to a nursing home in East Moriches, and died on January 18, 2001. Ken Yardley and Tony Pintauro arranged his burial in Oakland Cemetery. In 2003 local writer Annette Hinkle reviewed an exhibit of his seascapes at the Sag Harbor Historical Society:

> Much of Cappy's appeal lies in the fact that he painted the working class scenes of the waterfront…. His paintings depict a way of life that has disappeared over the course of a handful of years, and which has been replaced by the interests of a more elite population.

Even years later, in 2011, the American Hotel hosted a show of his whaling paintings and still treasures examples of his work. One of the delights of Terry Wallace's book is over 60 color photographs of Amundsen's paintings. The author notes on the last page, "Cappy Amundsen will forever live in Sag Harbor history."

Sag Harbor's Great Benefactor

She has been called "the early 20th century's major female philanthropist." She gave gifts to Sag Harbor that are part of the community's core — Pierson High School, John Jermain Memorial Library, Mashashimuet Park — as well as scores of smaller donations, like uniforms for the Phoenix Fire Company, repairs for the steeple of the old Presbyterian Church, a bell for Christ Episcopal Church and a new parsonage for the AME Zion church in Eastville. She summered in Sag Harbor after her husband died, but left in 1912 and never came back. Author Ruth Crocker describes this complicated woman in a biography simply titled *Mrs. Russell Sage*.

Born in Syracuse on September 8, 1828 to Joseph Slocum and Margaret Pierson Jermain, Margaret Olivia Slocum (she preferred the name Olivia) lived a long life, passing away on November 4, 1918. Her husband Russell Sage died in 1906 leaving her with over $75 million, equivalent to nearly $2 billion today. She was the second wife to Sage, a financier and a partner of famous railroad builder Jay Gould. Her maternal grandmother was Margaret Pierson of Bridgehampton who married John Jordan, an American patriot. He not only renounced his parents' Toryism, he changed his surname to Jermain when he moved here. (The author doesn't explain why he chose that particular name.) In the War of 1812, he was promoted to the rank of Major and commanded a fort in Sag Harbor.

Olivia's parents valued their ancestors, Abraham Pierson, first rector of Yale University, and educator Henry Pierson. They schooled Olivia at home until she attended the Troy Female Seminary, headed by Emma Willard, a famous feminist. For 20 years after graduation, Olivia supported herself by teaching in Syracuse and then in Philadelphia where she moved during the Civil War. She also worked there as a governess and volunteered at a military hospital.

After Russell Sage died, Olivia began 12 years of philanthropy to an amazing variety of causes. Besides significant gifts to Sag Harbor, she donated hundreds of thousands to Yale University and Cornell. She funded Holder Hall at Princeton, naming it for a Quaker ancestor. She also contributed sizeable amounts to Vassar, RPI, Syracuse University, and the National Training School for black teachers in Durham, NC. After 1912 she lived in her Fifth Avenue home and in Lawrence on the southwestern shore of Long Island. Much of her philanthropy was handled by the Russell Sage Foundation which she established in 1907 with a grant of $10 million. The foundation continues today, focusing on the improvement of social and living conditions in the U.S.

In 1908 Olivia purchased the former Huntting House, now the Whaling Museum, on Main Street and summered there until 1912. She then left and never returned. Why did she leave the village where she had been so influential? According to the author, Sage's philanthropy "put her in a Lady Bountiful relationship to the whole community."

Summer house for Mrs. Sage, now the Whaling Museum.

She was remembered as "bright and interesting" by some, and "a more contentious personality" by others.

A mistaken and misreported incident about her involvement in a school for factory workers "ended in recrimination, with the community in revolt against the reformer's uplift plans." Apparently Sag Harbor people were as feisty and outspoken in the early 1900s as they are today. Even worse was her discovery "that the contractors

213

for the high school had cheated her by substituting inferior building materials for the better ones she had paid for. One observer described Sag Harbor's inhabitants as 'unappreciative,' reported complaints that Sage had pauperized the community (by making it unwilling to shift for itself), and described vandalism against fixtures in the park."

The biographer says that over the years some six or seven thousand organizations asked her for money. Her advisor and lawyer Robert de Forest and her devoted secretary E. Lillian Todd fended off most approaches, but she gave far and wide, and quite eclectically — for several years every employee of Central Park received a Christmas gift, and she donated a small library of technical books to each of 258 firehouses in New York.

Her will left sizeable amounts to nineteen educational institutions, with other bequests to the NY Women's Hospital, the Children's Aid Society, the Metropolitan Museum of Art, the American Museum of Natural History, and a variety of religious causes.

Author Ruth Crocker says "philanthropy made concrete her best and worst impulses, her humane ideals and her prejudices, the ample generosity and the narrow-mindedness." Like all of us, Olivia had human failings, but she is best remembered for her great benevolence to Sag Harbor.

7

Homes and Places

The First Customs House in the U.S.

When it met in New York City in the summer of 1789, the First Congress of the infant United States found itself facing bankruptcy, with a debt of $77 million. Under the original Articles of Confederation, the Federal Government had no power to tax and had borrowed from France and Holland to finance the War of Independence. Congress and President George Washington responded quickly, passing the Tariff Act of July 4, 1789 which authorized collection of duties on goods coming into the new country. The recently established U.S. Customs Service named Sag Harbor a Federal Port of Entry and appointed Henry Packer Dering U.S. Customs Master. Henry was the son of Thomas Dering, a patriot who moved his family to Connecticut during the war to escape the British. While there, young Henry studied at Yale College and his framed diploma dated 1784 hangs today on the wall of the Customs House on Main Street in Sag Harbor.

Then busier than the port of New York City, Sag Harbor became a major source of the young country's finances. For the next three decades, Dering met vessels entering the harbor and levied duties on their cargos — 10 cents a gallon for Jamaican rum, two-and-a-half cents a pound for coffee, five cents a pound for wax or spermaceti candles, four cents a pound for cheese, two cents for soap, ten cents for snuff, and seven cents a pair for shoes, slippers or "goloshoes" made of leather. By 1835, customs revenues alone had reduced the national debt to zero.

Henry purchased what became the Customs House when he married Anna Fosdick in December 1793. The house then was at the corner of Union and Church Streets. He added to the home in 1806, probably because he and Anna raised nine children and he had also become Sag Harbor's first postmaster. In a letter to a relative, Anna wrote

The first Customs House in the United States.

Our leader George Washington has appointed my own dear husband Henry to serve as Customs Master here in Sag Harbor. The tea I buy will still be taxed (I chuckle to think my husband will be the one issuing that!) But I will sip that tasty brew more happily knowing that the money it brings in will help support our own new nation rather than go in some king's pocket across the ocean.

Martha Washington reportedly sent Anna a cutting from a box-wood bush at Mt. Vernon for planting in her yard. As a community leader, Henry invited David Frothingham to the village in May 1791 to establish our first newspaper, the *Long-Island Herald*.

The fully-furnished Customs House presents a fascinating look at the lifestyle of a prominent Long Island family between 1790 and 1820.

217

Just off the side entrance is the customs room furnished with Dering's work table and ledgers, and stand-up and roll-top desks made by Sag Harbor craftsmen. Henry raised a corner of the ceiling to accommodate a tall case-clock made of mahogany by William Claggett of Newport. Shutters on the inside of the windows slid shut for privacy as Dering did his official work.

Important guests, including James Fenimore Cooper, were welcomed into the elegant parlor with its Federal settee and Chippendale tea table and side chairs. A large chest, like others in the house, made up for lack of closets. In one corner is a violin and case crafted by Sag Harbor's Zebulon Elliott. Opposite stands another tall case-clock, this one built by Nathaniel Dominy of East Hampton.

The dining room is equally gracious, its mahogany table set with porcelain dishes carried as ballast in ships returning from China. Dinner guests sat in Duncan Phyfe chairs and ate with two-tined forks and engraved silver flatware. On a sideboard inside large glass enclosures are Sheffield lamps that could be lit with candles or whale oil. A "crumb cloth" protects the carpet and strips of wallpaper border the ceiling.

In the big kitchen fireplace a trammel suspended cast iron pots, pans and kettles over the flames. Early American versions of labor-saving devices helped servants prepare meals — a toasting rack and waffle maker, a tin reflector oven, a cabbage chopper, a wooden rolling pin with ivory handles, and a butter churn. In the pantry is a jar of brandied peaches put up in 1839. The kitchen has space for a spinning wheel, a baby-minder, a dish-drying rack, a pie-safe to keep out flies and children, and a tin bathtub shaped like a huge soup bowl.

In Henry's bedroom upstairs is a chest from his parent's home in Shelter Island and a fancy commode cabinet used when it was too dark or cold to get to the outhouse. A brass and copper bed warmer fought the chill, and on the floor next to the four-poster rests a pair of shoes, in those times neither right nor left but shaped by the feet of the wearer. The smaller children's rooms overflow with straw-filled, wrought iron sleigh-beds, toy furniture, doll cradles, and slates for school work.

When Henry Packer died in 1822 at age 58, he was succeeded as Customs Master by his son Henry Thomas. Almost all of the Derings are buried in Oakland Cemetery. By the 1940s, the once grand house had become an abandoned derelict and was about to be demolished. The Olde Sagg Harbour Committee appealed for help to Charles Edison, former New Jersey governor and son of the famous inventor, who summered in the Hannibal French House on Main Street. Edison loved Sag Harbor and donated part of his property as a new site for the Customs House. It took three days to make the careful move, with the lighting company detaching overhead wires along the way. The Society for Preservation of Long Island Antiquities studied the building's original interior design and located a large number of family pieces, aided by Anna Dering's own household inventories. In 1971 after a three-year restoration, Sag Harbor's Customs House was designated a National Landmark.

This summer when you're wondering what to do with those weekend guests, give them a peek at local history. The Customs House is open weekends beginning Memorial Day, daily in July and August, and weekends from Labor Day to Columbus Day.

Harbor History in Oakland Cemetery

Most of us shy away from cemeteries, perhaps not wanting to be reminded of our mortality. But a walk through Oakland Cemetery on Jermain Avenue is surprisingly pleasant, especially in the informed company of Ernest Schade, a long-time Harborite who treasures everything about the village. Oakland's mossy acres are beautiful, even though the graves show their age, some stones covered with lichen, a few broken or fallen over. But the mood beneath towering Oak trees is peaceful and soft. Poet Margaret Brehman wrote, "I have stood alone and quiet in the filtered sunlight beneath the old trees, listening to the sighing wind and the chattering of birds...."

World-famous ballet master George Balanchine felt the same way. He is buried here because he "liked the look of it." Ballerina Alexandra Danilova, who left Russia with Balanchine in 1924, also chose a resting place in Oakland, not far from Balanchine's grave. Actor and film-maker Spalding Gray came here in January 2004, his gravestone a rough rock inscribed in part, "An American Original, Troubled, Inner-Directed and Can-Not Type." Two unexpected residents were Iranian princes — Manucher and Abol Bashar Farmanfarmaian. Their family had fled Iran after the downfall of the Shah in 1979. Educated in England and the United States, the brothers built successful business careers. A devoted sailor, Abol spent vacations in Sag Harbor and sailed his boat in local waters. When he died in 1991, his family laid him to rest in Oakland, and when his brother died years later, he was buried alongside Abol.

Other names may be familiar, such as novelists Nelson Algren and William Gaddis, but the real fascination and history of Oakland is in the illustrious, legendary families that are buried here. If you have looked at all into Sag Harbor history you will recognize family clusters marked Huntting, Havens, Corwin, Fordham, Latham, Hildreth, French, Babcock, Topping, Halsey, Cook, Glover, Conkling, Bill, Finckenor. Most of the gravestones are fairly humble. Only two mausoleums were built in the cemetery, the largest a 14-ft. square, granite tomb marked "Fahys," the man who moved his watchcase factory to Sag Harbor and married a local girl.

A November 1989 *New York Times* article by Kathleen Parrish said the Oakland acres "were laid out in 1840, but the oldest grave, moved from the Old Burying Ground next to the Whalers Church, is that of Hezekiah Jennings, dated 1767." Historian Dorothy Zaykowski

Oakland Cemetery on Jermain Avenue.

explains that in the mid-19th century as Madison Street was being graded and paved, it was feared that caskets might tumble into the street from the over-crowded Old Burying Ground, and in 1860 a number of graves were moved to the new cemetery.

Captain David Hand, a whaling captain who died in 1840, is surrounded by the graves of his five wives. He wrote a puckish epitaph, "Behold ye living passing by, how thick the partners of one husband lie." Perhaps the most famous memorial in Oakland is a white marble shaft representing the broken mast of a ship, inscribed on its base "Entombed in the ocean, they live in our memory." The names of six Sag Harbor whaleship captains who lost their lives in the dangerous business are engraved on its sides.

There is sad history in the graves of men who fought in too many wars, from the War of Independence to conflicts centuries later far from home. A large stone is inscribed "To the memory of Eugene

Smith French, Son of Stephen B and Mary A French, Born at Sag Harbor January 23, 1862, Died on the Field of Battle at Caloocan, Philippine Islands Friday February 23, 1899." A new grave is that of Lance Corporal Jordan C. Haerter of the U.S. Marine Corps, a son of Sag Harbor, who was killed defending fellow Marines in Iraq and was awarded the Navy Cross for heroism.

Grave in Oakland Cemetery of renowned choreographer George Balanchine.

There is history too in a grave marked Olive L. Pharaoh "Queen of the Montaukett Indians." Here and there in Oakland are flowers, some artificial, and little American flags stuck in the ground. Small stones sit on top of some graves, probably placed with a prayer and a memory. Only the main path is black-topped, otherwise the ground is gravel, grass and moss.

According to Ken Yardley of Yardley & Pino there are some 3,000 occupants here, but the village fathers who acquired the acreage looked far ahead — on its southern edge is an undeveloped section, providing room for more Harborites, or for people who just like the look of the place.

It might be wise to make a reservation now.

The Genius Who Built Revered Clocks

We regale visitors to the village with tales about our whaling ships, our historic homes, and the nation's first Customs House, but we seem to overlook a nationally renowned 19th century scientist who was born, raised and worked in Sag Harbor. Ephraim Niles Byram, among many other accomplishments, built magnificent tower clocks for the U.S. Military Academy at West Point, New York's City Hall, London's Stone Church, and our own Methodist Church on Madison Street. He also built a clock for the Virginia Military Institute that became the subject of controversy 160 years after it was installed.

Byram was born in Sag Harbor on November 25, 1809, to Eliab and Cynthia Clark Byram. According to Russella J. Hazard, writing in the October 1956 issue of the *Long Island Forum*, Ephraim grew up a quiet and serious boy, perhaps because he had to survive among seven children. He left school early, finding it difficult to follow set rules, and educated himself in science, mechanics, and astronomy. At age 25, he created a mechanical model of the solar system, called an orrery. A Sag Harbor newspaper, the *Republican Watchman,* reported in March 1836 that the orrery would be set up in the village Arsenal, with an accompanying lecture by Byram. Later the American Institute of New York requested his creation to be exhibited in Manhattan and awarded Ephraim its Gold Medal.

Ephraim moved on to designing and building clocks, telescopes, even musical organs, and continued to take meteorological observations. His great interest in navigational instruments aboard whaling and cargo ships that docked in Sag Harbor led him to study celestial navigation. Between 1842 and 1866 he repaired and manufactured chronometers and compasses for over 70 ships sailing from Long Wharf.

He built his first clock for the tower of Sag's Methodist Church in 1838. Years later church trustees declared that the clock varied less than three minutes a year. As his fame spread, he built clocks for churches in Newton, Mass.; La Grange, Georgia; London, England; and for the 220-foot spire of Louisville, Kentucky's Baptist Church. The clock for New York's City Hall featured glass dials seven feet in diameter.

It was his clock built for VMI in 1852 that has created a horological kerfuffle 160 years later. Apparently, during the Civil War when Union Army General David Hunter gutted the Lexington, Virginia military college, Byram's clock vanished and later emerged, a spoil of war, in the tower of the Warren County Courthouse in Belvidere, New Jersey. A couple of years ago when Warren County decided to convert the clock to an electronic mechanism, experts expressed skepticism that the courthouse clock is indeed Byram's VMI clock. The *Warren County Express-Times* has covered the story extensively, perhaps not momentous news but things do get a little slow in the summer. VMI is conducting its own research and if it turns out that the Warren County clock originally was built for the school, it will be repatriated to the south. Stay tuned.

According to the *Guide to Sag Harbor Landmarks, Homes & History*, Byram designed his own house on Jermain Avenue, west of Oakland Cemetery, in the manner of an Italianate villa with a campanile where he set up telescopes and hung pendulums. He built his clocks in a shop behind the house.

In 1857 Byram married Cornelia J. Pierce of Elmira, NY (no word on how they met), and they raised three children. The same year he built a clock for the U.S. Military Academy at West Point, his account book reading "Completed Nov. 1857. Set running in tower of Collegiate Hall, May 1, 1858. Price $940." In 1929 an academy publication reported "...the dial was of wood and measured five feet across. The hands and numerals were also of wood...for 72 years the clock has given satisfactory service."

Byram made a grandfather clock for his own Sag Harbor home in 1869. Many years later his daughter Loretta willed the clock to the

Famous clock-maker Ephraim Byram built and tested tower clocks in the campanile of his distinctive home.

John Jermain Memorial Library and it was set in the library's main entrance hall. Director Catherine Creedon reassured us that during the library's expansion, the 145-year old clock received therapy at Netusil Jewelers in Rocky Point and will have a prominent place in the completed building.

In his last years, Byram settled down as a bookbinder and collected volumes on science and mechanics. He passed away on June 27, 1881, ending a life of genius and achievement, deserving to be celebrated by his native village. A pedestal topped by a globe marks the Byram family plot in Oakland cemetery.

✳ ✳ ✳

Preserving History in Sag Harbor

On Thanksgiving Day we give thanks for the many things we love about Sag Harbor. The human scale of Main Street that draws visitors all year-round. The elegant or humble 19th century houses on the side streets. The open welcome of Long Wharf. The Whaling Museum rich with nautical fascinations. The boats that grace the lovely waterfront. The steeple-deprived Whalers Church. Mashashimuet Park. The movie house with its iconic sign. The Variety Store. Boatyards. The Cove. Oakland Cemetery. So many sweet elements that make a lovely village.

That's why we worry about it. We worry about new development that might be out of character. We worry about new arrivals who consider a Sag house an investment, want to core it out, enlarge it and put in a pool. Thankfully, there have always been watchful groups of village lovers who might, just might, hold back the newness tide, or at least control it, because it can't be stopped completely. Writer-photographer Stephen Longmire in his 2007 book, *Keeping Time In Sag Harbor*, marking the 300th anniversary of the village, wrote,

> "An architectural treasure-trove, Sag Harbor retains a chronicle of early American buildings, high style and vernacular, thanks to its long history of economic ups and downs.... The village's homes are histories that more or less stay put, and they have helped me tell its story.... Buildings are time capsules, full of the lives they have held.

The Old Whaler's Church lost its steeple in the hurricane of 1938.

Longmire's photos are beautiful enough for one of those oversized coffee-table volumes, but his writing too is a delight — the thoughtful introduction, the heartfelt interviews with Sag Harbor people, and the section "Where Houses Are Historians" that poses important questions. On the delicate balance between historic preservation and judicious development, Longmire cautions about "the predicament of a place that could be loved to death."

The book is enlivened by Longmire's mother Joyce Egginton who collected perceptive observations, like this from Carol Williams, "I believe a lot of people end up staying in my village because of its mesmerizing street pattern.... With such a map, every errand is an adventure." David Lee who came here in 1948 worries also "...there are no affordable homes for those who work here, and hardly any place to build them." David Bray who worked in real estate remarked, "There are very few big homes here, and some very wealthy people live in rather modest homes. To buy into this village, with homes so close, you have to be bitten by the Sag Harbor bug."

Over the last century, Sag Harbor has been blessed by citizens who appreciated the history of the village and worked to preserve it. Josephine Bassett, interviewed in 1976, was a founder of the Old Sagg-Harbour Committee. She and her allies convinced Charles Edison, son of the famous inventor and former Governor of New Jersey, to move the old Customs House to his property alongside the Hannibal French House on Main Street. "We ladies took on the project and hung on by our fingernails until it was done."

As far back as 1966, the federal government recognized the value of historic places and passed the National Historic Preservation Act "to preserve the historical and cultural foundation of the nation as a living part of community life." In 1971 the Suffolk County Planning Department stated, "It is quite obvious that Sag Harbor has the character of a national historic district, a living part of American history. Though it is a small town, Sag Harbor is as much a part of the national scene as the French Quarter in New Orleans or Greenwich Village in New York."

In 1973, the local historic district was entered in the State and National Historic Register and now every application for a building permit must be reviewed by the Board of Historic Preservation and Architectural Review. Former Chairman C. Scott Brown says the board encourages owners contemplating renovations or expansions in the historic district to meet early in the planning process. The purpose — to assist "the architect or developer in arriving at a design that shows a thoughtful relationship to neighboring buildings and is as much in keeping as possible with the scale, materials, and visual feelings of the village as a whole." A Certificate of Appropriateness is required for anyone who wishes to alter the exterior of a building within the historic district. (The Architectural Review Board is now headed by Anthony Brandt.)

Longmire commented recently that Sag Harbor's preservation status is an opportunity to define the community's values and hold new arrivals to them. We'd add that government is only as good as the citizens supporting it, and we give thanks for the people who love Sag Harbor and guard its precious stock of history. But it's a never ending battle.

About the Author

Jim Marquardt has been a regular columnist for the award-winning *Sag Harbor Express* newspaper for the last ten years. He has written about local history, nature, immigration, personality profiles, travel, humor, and sailing.

For twenty-five years he was president of Marquardt & Roche Inc., Advertising/Public Relations in Stamford, Connecticut.

Jim also worked for New York City communications firms and corporations as an advertising/promotion copywriter, publicity writer, and magazine editor.

For several years he reviewed fiction for *Dan's Papers*, a well-known weekly periodical published on the East End of Long Island.

Jim graduated from St. Peter's University in New Jersey with a Bachelor of Arts in English Literature. Years later, he returned to teach a compulsory freshman writing course at this Jesuit institution.

He has written nonfiction articles for magazines and newspapers. His fiction has appeared in the *North Atlantic Review* and the *East Hampton Star.*